After the Buzzer
Transitioning Your Sports Skills to Life

By Andrew Wingard

Heather,

Thank You for this great opportunity.
I hope you enjoy!

R.A.W. Form Publishing

Youngstown, Ohio

After the Buzzer: Transitioning Your Sports Skills
to Life COPYRIGHT © 2020

Printed in the United States of America

ISBN: 978-0-578-79785-4

Cover by Rob W.

Edited by Cori Wamsley, www.coriwamsley.com

This book is dedicated to Coach Doug Brotherton and his family and all the Coach Brotherton's around the world. Thank you!

TABLE OF CONTENTS

FOREWORD

Athletes all around the world are competing and laying their bodies on the line for the sport they love. Many of us grow up with ambitions to make it to the next level of our sport, but only a few are granted that opportunity. Even fewer make it to the pinnacle of that sport.

Some of us, however, just play sports because we want to spend time with our friends. As I got older, the game developed a deeper meaning for me. I started to not only play for my friends, but I started to play for my family. I played to make my family proud. I played for something my family could hold onto. I played for pride in my last name because basketball gave me that opportunity. That's when it became bigger than a game.

My brothers were not bad kids, but following in their footsteps at school was not always pleasant. Teachers would get to my name at the bottom of the attendance sheet and say, "Another Wingard?" I never asked if their comments were negative or positive. I knew my brothers were not angels. I grew up with them, and we often shared the same end of my father's belt. I spent most of my teenage life yearning to correct the impressions, and basketball was a great way to start.

In the fall of 2003, I was a freshman at Bridgeport High School (Bridgeport, Mich.). When I received my first report card as a high school student, I wasn't too proud of it. At that low moment, I decided to set out on my mission, spurred by the question people sometimes asked me—"How are you so different from your brothers?" In reality, I was not that different from them at all. They are my brothers. They are my best friends. I just happened to have basketball in my life. I chose to use that to change the narrative. I chose to express myself in a different manner. Basketball was the way.

My energy around the game started to change. I wasn't playing just for fun anymore. I had more at stake. I was playing for my school. I was playing for my brothers who showed up for practice every day with me. I was playing for my close friends. I was playing for the community. I was playing for my family. And most importantly, I was playing for my mom.

My mom told me a story after the first game of my senior season at Bridgeport High School. She had been watching in the stands as we played Frankenmuth High School, our rival down the road. Early in the game, nerves were still high, and I missed a layup. Someone near my mom said, "He's trash." Surprisingly, it was someone there rooting for Bridgeport. At the end of the game, though, I hit the buzzer-beater that gave us the victory. My mom said she turned around and said to that person, "How about that?" If you know Mrs. Wingard, you know she is probably the humblest human being on earth. Very rarely will she step out into the light. When she told me about that, I knew, at that moment, it was bigger than a game.

What did I really learn from basketball? How was basketball more than a game? And most importantly, could I convert what I learned from basketball to my life outside of the gym?

Colleges such as Texas Tech and Clemson hire professionals specifically to handle preparing athletes for life after competitive sport and helping young adults embrace their journey to attach meaning to it. These professionals are just as important as their actual coach. They are vital to athletic departments and the well-being of campus overall. Coaches do not allow athletes to show up to the game without practicing day in and day out. Professional life coaches on campus play the same role for students. Why would we think students don't need the same practice as they prepare to leave the competitive sport world? It takes time and practice to get ready for life away from the game you love.

Three out of four former student-athletes report having trouble retiring from competitive sport, according to one NCAA study. How does a student-athlete do that when their department lacks a big enough budget to hire this type of professional? You must use the resources you have access to: alumni, local professionals, college administration, faculty, and peers.

After the Buzzer is not just a book; it is my personal journal. A journal of how I made sense of my journey and how I use that knowledge every day. My purpose was to share my journey with anyone transitioning or preparing to make a transition. Whether you are transitioning from competitive sport or transitioning into a new job, it takes time and practice to transition. Working in intercollegiate athletics and in Franklin Simpson High School in Franklin, Ky., during graduate school, I learned there was a common theme amongst students—Students have trouble transitioning into life. Whether they are athletes or regular students. We all struggle the same.

By writing this book, I wanted to leave notes about my life that could possibly serve communities like Franklin because life is ever-changing, and we are constantly transitioning. I made a tough decision my junior year of college to stop playing the game I loved, competitively, and focus on academics. I recently took a job in a new field with little experience in the area. I hope this journal serves as a small playbook for those preparing to transition or for anyone currently in transition.

INTRODUCTION

"Leadership is the ability to unlock people's potential to become better." - Bill Bradley

Raw. Not polished, finished, or processed. Lacking experience or understanding, untested, inexperienced, or unfinished. Something with potential for improvement, development, or elaboration. Very young with the ability to surpass actual skills at the moment. We are all born into this world very raw as we leave our mother's womb, lacking the experience we need to be successful. We figure out those elements of life as time goes on. Our understanding of the world around us develops as our experiences grow. The parental figures tell the children "no," but we do not understand why they are keeping us from climbing up the dining room table. We do not see the dangers because we are inexperienced as infants. We have little fear when it comes to exploring the unknown as infants.

Whether from our parents, siblings, cousins, or friends of the family, we receive help in developing the raw areas of our lives. In March 2006, my journey began. It was my junior year of high school, and we had finished the worst basketball season of my life. We were bounced out of the tournament in the district finals matchup against Hemlock. That's when my head coach presented an opportunity for a few of us to try out for the Central Michigan All-Stars travel basketball team.

It was my first time playing travel ball. We had a local team in Saginaw, but honestly, I was not talented enough to compete on that team. I was thrilled about the opportunity now in front of me. The entire course of my life would be changed by those three months with the Central Michigan All-Stars. Coach Doug Brotherton took a chance on me. Coach Brotherton saw something in me I did not necessarily see in myself.

Coach Brotherton saw *rawness* and a young man with potential for improvement and development. After a while, I recognized what Coach Brotherton saw. I did not have much confidence in any area of my life at that age. Coach put in a massive number of hours *forming* me that summer—molding, shaping, developing my talent, as well as my mind—and I will forever be grateful for his time. Coach Brotherton started as my coach, but he later became a big brother, mentor, and a dear friend.

R.A.W. Form is my personal brand. Coach Doug Brotherton is the true definition of R.A.W. Form. He introduced me to a structured transition offense with different options. Transition offense also happened to be my strongest attribute in the game of basketball. That is why I titled the first chapter of this book "Transition." It's a good place to start.

CHAPTER ONE
TRANSITION

"It is when we are in transition that we are most completely alive." *William Bridges*

I found that quote by William Bridges sensational for this chapter and the entire book. Whether we are a basketball player in transition or an adult transitioning into a new career field, we are most alive in either case. Eager to get moving. Eager to excel. Eager for the opportunity. Excited about the possibilities that transition has to offer.

The term "transition" has a few different meanings in basketball. "Transition" can be used for both the offensive and defensive sides of the ball. Most of this book will be reflecting on the idea of transition and how it played a role in my life, as well as looking at transitioning at different times in my life.

Transition is the process of changing. Do you remember the show *Pokémon*? It was one of the highlights of my childhood. Pokémon, the creatures on the show, would "evolve," which reminds me of how we transition and evolve during our time on earth.

Pokémon get to evolve in a few different ways. One, they evolve through battling. Two, they evolve through friendship. Three, they evolve when they come in contact with certain stones or items. Pokémon are extremely excited when they evolve. Their trainers are normally excited as well. When I played the Pokémon video game, I was always extremely excited when one of my Pokémon evolved during the course of the game. I knew, through battles and tests, they would eventually transition to something bigger and faster.

Much like Pokémon, we transition and evolve through battling, friendship, and coming into contact with items. Whether we are battling for a position on the team, for a promotion at work, to close a big deal, or even while trying to pick up on a new hobby, we are constantly evolving and transitioning. We evolve through friendships because our loved ones help us grow to reach our true potential. Our loved ones push us, and they hold us accountable. Our loved ones comfort us and help us to get over turmoil and pain. We also evolve when we come into contact with certain items like an evolution stone in Pokémon. Sure, evolution stones work instantly in Pokémon, but life isn't that easy for us. We can grow from coming into contact with items such as healthy food, books, or weights, to name a few.

Transition in basketball is the process of changing from defense to offense quickly. In a structured transition offense, there are normally options that the ball handler has to read. A transition offense can be slow, with a walking-it-up-the-court type of play or an aggressive, fast-break scenario. The aggressive fast-break scenario was all I really knew growing up. The goal was to get easy baskets, wear down the opposing team, and keep the defense on their heels—backpedaling and unsure, which keeps them unbalanced and easy to attack.

I was introduced to a more controlled and strategic transition offense my junior year of high school. I was new to the scene of AAU Basketball, and I was traveling with the Central Michigan All-Stars. The fast break took on a different meaning that spring. We still pushed the ball aggressively at times, but Coach Brotherton's transition had an overall goal with many options.

Transition with the Central Michigan All-Stars was a more strategic attack, and it was highly effective. That team didn't have a ton of "athletes," but we could put the ball in the basket in a variety of ways. His style of transition was perfect for our group of guys. It also became one of the foundations of my young adult life.

As we grow older, we naturally transition, whether we are transitioning into college, a different major in college your sophomore year, a new operating system at work, a new job, or even a new city. I see every day as a new day to evolve and learn something new. The path of constant learning will lead you down a path of constant transition, which in turn will hopefully help you be a better you. And like Coach's structured transition, we have options in life. Sometimes we make good decisions and, other times, not so good.

The fundamental principles of an effective transition offense in basketball have some of the same rules in our daily lives.

Rules of Transition

1. Coach has to Assign Roles

You can't run an effective transition offense without practicing it every day and defining expectations for your players. It is not something players pick up and do automatically at the start. Every coach that runs any sort of transition/fast-break offensive scheme spends time practicing. It gets better over time as the players start to gel. The coach usually assigns each player a number and route. But understanding your role in the offense doesn't mean you only know your role. It's important to understand the flow of the game and where everyone is supposed to be on the court, especially if you are the main ball handler. It is your job as a player to understand your role in the offense. It is also your job to know where your team is. This increases the effectiveness of the fast-break. That is why teams that have spent more time together run these types of offenses so well.

In basketball, there are so many transition offenses, and we can't assume just because we know the expectations and route of one, that we know the expectations and route for every transition offensive scheme. For the fast-break or transition offense to work efficiently, everyone must know what their job is. One breakdown and you give the defense a chance to recover or possibly force a turnover. By assigning players a number and designed route, coaches reduce the number of decisions each player must make. Basketball is an up-tempo game. Making decisions on your own in that kind of environment is tough when you are just starting out with the concept of any transition offense.

Making decisions in life is very similar to making decisions in transition, whether you are acting as the coach, the ball handler, the wing, or even the post. Some decisions are just flat out hard to make. It doesn't matter how much experience you have. *Do I push the ball as hard as I can and force the issue? Do I push the ball and look back for the trailer? Do I advance the ball ahead to the streaking wing? Do I hit the post streaking down the middle of the floor? Should I go on a date with that guy or girl? Should I transfer schools? Should I stop playing the game I love and focus on school? Should I forgive that person? Should I help that person? Should I make that church my home? Should I move to Spain?* These are all examples of transition questions that we face in basketball and life.

I would be lying if I told you I didn't turn the ball over at times. That is the risk you face when you are in transition. All we can do is try to make the best decision that we can at that time. Unlike basketball, we don't have to make decisions on a dime in our personal lives. The way I make decisions now is different than how I would make them when I was 23. I partner prayer, friend's guidance, Mikael Krogerus and Roman Tschappeler's *The Decision Book: Fifty Models for Strategic Thinking*, and many other resources. I use everything I have possible to make decisions now.

When I started traveling with the basketball team, I put myself in a position to meet people from every background possible. Everyone was unique and brought something special to my life team, but I had to know how to manage those relationships.

We are the head coach of our lives, which means we are responsible for assigning those around us to certain roles. We also need to understand the role we play for others. Employers lose employees and relationships fail when expectations are not defined, so the expectations and roles need to be clearly explained and established. It is vital that you know what your role and expectations are from your boss. Ask your friends what they expect of you. Ask your partner what they expect from you. Like basketball and work, if these roles are not clearly defined, the offense would have no structure and would not be effective, and the work environment would be toxic. This isn't only for our benefit but also for us to benefit them.

Never forget you are the acting head coach. Your players, friends, co-workers, and associates are only going to be as good as the positions you put them in. If you have a friend that is good at listening, you probably don't want to position that person far away from you. If you have a friend that lies and feeds you bad energy, you may not want them too close to you. You must decide where people go in your transition offense. This doesn't mean that when you assign a role to someone it won't expand or change over time. That is the beauty of transition. Transition is change! The special players can play multiple positions in any transition offense scheme. The special people in our lives will do the same.

2.   You have to be in Good Conditioning

Coach Carter, a popular basketball movie, has a very funny scene, in which many basketball players can relate. If you have not seen the movie, Samuel L. Jackson took over coaching a team in Richmond, Calif. While preparing for their first game, he told the players, "I know you are concerned with us not running any offense during practice. But what did we do during practice?" The players responded, "Run." Coach Carter responded, "That's exactly what I want you to do. Run!"

It does not matter what style of transition offense you run in basketball if you aren't well-conditioned—not just conditioned physically but conditioned mentally. The offense will not be beneficial to your team. As I mentioned earlier in this chapter, basketball is an up-tempo game. It can take a toll on you if you are not prepared properly. When you are fatigued physically, you are more likely to make poor decisions. That is why being conditioned is so important. Transition is the process of changing from defense to offense quickly. Transition in life is the process of changing. You can't transition and lack physical and mental conditioning, and the only way to condition both is through practice.

Basketball and life require an enormous amount of energy. From dating to dealing with family situations. We need energy to get through the game of life. Being well-conditioned helps us make better decisions, prevent injuries, and run longer. When you make better decisions, you get promotions. When you can prevent injuries, you are more effective for your team, co-workers, friends, and family.

When you are well-conditioned, you can push through when everyone else is giving up, you do not have to slow the ball down after a defensive rebound, and you can attack the basket and life in a positive, aggressive manner. When you are well-conditioned, you make one more sales call at the end the day, you write one more page in your journal before bed, and you can push through the darkest of nights.

## 3.	Be in Control

Coaches of kids and young adults must find an equal balance of teaching an aggressive transition style of play and being in control, which can be difficult.

As a basketball player, if you are not in control, the easy point opportunities become less effective, which leads to turnovers and missed opportunities to score. When you are out of control in life, you make bad decisions and miss opportunities. When you are not in control, you make bad decisions about who you should be dating. When you are not in control, you play on your phone during work instead of focusing on your goals. When you are not in control, you make bad decisions about your new diet plan. When you are not in control, you agree to attend happy hour instead of going to the gym after work. When you are not in control, you turn on Netflix instead writing that business plan or song you have been wanting to write. When you are not in control, you choose to stay up late playing video games instead of studying. When you are not in control, you spend your morning scrolling through your social media accounts instead of meditating or listening to a Ted Talk podcast. When you are not in control, you engage in bad habits. When you are not in control, you spend money instead of saving for your dream vacation.

When I think about not being in control. I think about the concept of the Virtuous Cycle. I was introduced to the concept from a motivational speaker online and have heard it referred to by many people over the years. The idea behind a Virtuous Cycle is to create an upward spiral versus a downward spiral. Positive actions lead to positive results. The virtuous cycle helps us create momentum. Momentum is great for winning games in basketball and great for our lives. Daily positive actions or decisions can lead to other positive actions, decisions, and results.

The good news about transition in this situation is it is only one play. We can't be scared to fail and make mistakes. It is easy to get down on ourselves when we make mistakes and fall. Being in control means getting up when you are too weak to stand physically or mentally. Being in control means moving on to the next play. Being in control means lifting up your teammates, your family, and your friends in tough times. Being in control means accepting fear but not letting it control you.

Being in control does not mean we have it all together. Being in control means understanding there is no such thing as perfection. We make mistakes! We miss shots! We turn the ball over! Pick your head up, and move on to the next play.

Chapter One Wrap-Up: Transition

1. After reading this chapter, what does transition mean to you?

2. Who have you assigned roles to in your life? (Ex: Who do you confide in?)

3. Do you condition your body and mind? What ways do you condition yourself for transition?

4. What is one positive habit you can start this week to create a Virtuous Cycle?

CHAPTER TWO
FOLLOW THROUGH

"There is no secret to success. But there is a system to success." – Anonymous

Basketball Scenario: A basketball player is hit hard by the defender while attacking the basket. The referee blows his whistle and calls a foul on the defender. The offensive player steps to the line to shoot a pair of free throws. They step to the line, take a few dribbles, and shoot the ball. The player misses the shot, and you hear a yell from across the gym, "Follow through!"

The follow-through is an essential step in shooting a basketball. One coach says, "Holding your follow-through solves a multitude of shooting problems. This simple movement helps you maintain good basketball shooting technique without even thinking about it." Coaches all around the world emphasize the importance of following through.

Please do not take this chapter out of context. Multiple mechanics are involved when you talk about shooting a basketball. In this chapter, I am only focusing on the art of following through.

I would like to believe following through is essential in our daily walk. Following through is linked to success across many sports. Not only does holding your follow-through improve your success rate on the court, but in the professional realm, follow-through is vital to your survival. The concepts are very similar and equally important.

One afternoon, a co-worker from a different division in the department stopped by the ticket office, where I worked. He asked, "What are you up to Andrew?" I responded with, "Following up with some people." He said, "That is good stuff. Not very many people take time to follow up." Following through (or following up) requires a human presence. Studies reveal that sales professionals agree that a lack of follow-through is the primary element missing when sales are not keeping pace with leads generated.

Following through shows that you are fully committed. Committed to the proper shooting technique. Committed to helping your favorite non-profit. Committed to helping your local Chamber of Commerce. Committed to building relationships in business. Committed to establishing great partnerships. Committed to developing a strong and healthy relationship with your significant other. Committed to following through with a customer to ensure you are serving them at the highest level possible. Committed to completing your goals. Committed to execution. Committed to being a better man or woman. Committed to changing the path for your family.

It is very easy for us to become committed to things that may not be beneficial to our growth. It is easy to be committed to binge watching your favorite television show versus going to work out. It is easier to not follow-through and call the person you met from the networking event the evening before. It takes effort to follow through on what you need to do. It takes zero effort and energy to do nothing.

My first college football game day with Youngstown State University was steaming hot, as most football games are in August or early September. I handled that game day the same way I handled game day at Texas Tech University and Tulane University: I went on seat visits to meet our supporters. Leading up to the season, as I talked to our supporters over the phone, I mentioned that I would stop by their seats to introduce myself, so that is what I did on game day. I made it a point to follow through on that promise. One season ticket holder noted that she was not expecting a visit from me. She thought it was a customer service ploy. I often reflect on her comment. Her expectation of me following through on my commitment was slim to none. I personally find that very concerning.

As professionals, we are so lax in our follow-through that people become numb to the idea of others keeping their word. I believe it should be the other way around. The expectation should be to follow-up on our commitments. What transpired from my extra effort that game day was a great relationship with one of our supporters. The relationship blossomed and flourished, all because I followed through and spent two minutes introducing myself at the home opener.

Make sure you always follow through with a colleague or customer. Be a man or woman of your word. The follow-through is vital when closing out games. One of the most iconic follow-through photos is that of Michael Jordan. Every sports fan has seen that special photo of Michael Jordan closing out the game and his basketball career against the Utah Jazz.

Following through is equally important as we go through life together. Many sales professionals will agree that following through after a sale is just as important if not more important than the actual sale itself. Following through with your supporters or partners builds trust and loyalty. When trust and loyalty are established, people are more willing to share their positive experience with family and friends. You become of value to your supporters and partners. By cultivating the relationship, you open the door to other opportunities like referrals. That does not happen if you do not create a strong relationship.

When we do not follow through on our commitments in life, we can create bad habits and a negative or downward spiral. Lack of commitment on any team is detrimental to the success of the team and the individual. So, when you think about your responsibility as a teammate. When you do not hold yourself accountable to following through, you are hurting your team and, more importantly, doing yourself a disservice. That is why coaches and strength and conditioning professionals put such an emphasis on working hard during the off-season. A lack of commitment and following through can impact those around us negatively. Following through is a good habit, and it needs to be practiced daily. Like anything, it takes work to establish it as a habit. Whether it is a good or bad habit. John Wooden says, "The best way to improve the team is to improve yourself." The best way to improve yourself is to create an upward spiral of positive energy and create positive habits.

Following through will show if you are truly committed to yourself. Following through will show if you are committed to serving your supporters and partners. Working in the service industry, following through plays a vital role in the day-to-day operations.

Following through means planning and setting goals. When I moved to Wilson, N.C., to attend Charis Prep School, my goal was to become a collegiate basketball player at the Division I level. But I could not reach that goal without a proper plan and following through on that plan. So, I put together a plan. I asked myself, "How can I be successful, and how can I become a Division I athlete?" I decided to follow all of the guys who were getting prepared to play at that level. Whatever they did, I did! Wherever they went, I went! That was my plan, and that is what I was committed to.

A very similar situation transpired as I was getting ready to graduate from Saginaw Valley State University (University Center, Mich.). I wanted to be the best customer service/business professional in the world. I loved business and service. So, I asked myself again, "How can I become the best in the world? Who can show me the ropes?" That is when I applied to the Disney Internship Program. Thankfully, I was accepted into the program.

Then I asked myself another question, "How do I make the best use of this experience?" I put together another plan of action:

- Never miss a day of work.
- Pick up extra shifts.
- Ask a ton of questions.
- Ask the right questions.
- Volunteer when I can.
- Build as many relationships as possible.

This was another set of goals I needed to follow through on for me to be successful. Once these goals were in place, it was up to me to follow through on my commitments. I wish I could say it was easy all the time. I was tempted many times to miss a day of work, and when you live in Orlando, Fla., that is a very easy thing to do.

At the end of the first marking period of my freshman year at Bridgeport High School, report cards were handed out. It was not a shock to me that I failed two classes. It was more shocking realizing that I would not be able to play basketball my freshman year. For the first time in a long time, I would not be able to partake in the game I loved. I ended up failing another class that year and that put me back in ninth grade standing the following year.

Even though I was not eligible to play basketball my freshman year, the freshman coach at that time gave me an opportunity to still be a part of the team. I am grateful for him not giving up on me. The coach could have easily dismissed me when he found out I was ineligible, but he did not. That saved me from digging myself into an even deeper hole. It kept me active and was exactly what I needed to get my head right.

During Christmas break, we had an open gym, and we scrimmaged the junior varsity team. At that moment, I realized I needed to make a change. Missing a basketball season was not an option going forward. I wish I could say I completely focused on my studies so I could play, but not much changed in the years following. I walked a thin line between passing and academic probation. I played basketball each year following but by the skin of my teeth.

My lack of commitment to my goals of staying eligible put me up against the ropes as I prepared for graduation. My lack of commitment had me fighting upstream with a strong current. I had just finished my first summer ever of travel AAU Basketball with Doug Brotherton and the Central Michigan All-Stars. It was the experience I needed to keep me from drowning. I love Doug, but I wish he had come into my life sooner. "Better late than never," though, right? That summer lit a fire in me I did not know existed. Doug gave me hope. That opportunity opened my eyes. That opportunity gave me new energy.

After high school, I was so far behind that I could not pay to get into college. No way would any admissions professional let in a kid with a 1.6 grade point average. I remember sitting down with Coach P of Charis Prep in his office. He said, "Son, there is nothing you can do with your grades. You only have one option." So, I pursued and attacked that option. I entered junior college, and my journey as a college player began.

When I started college, I made sure I followed through on my academic pursuit. Basketball was important, but not as important as proving to myself I could graduate from college. When we would travel for games, I would study, read, and do any homework that needed completed. You could argue that academics were more important to me than basketball at that time of my life. I still had my goal of becoming a Division I basketball player, but I knew I needed every credit to count for the NCAA clearinghouse.

Habits have a way of reshaping us. Whether those are good or bad habits. Following through happened to be a good habit for me, and twelve years later, I can share how that turned my life around.

Whether at work or in your personal life, following through is essential. It does not matter where you are when you hear the yell, "Follow through!" You can be sitting in a gym, your office, at home, at church, driving down the street, or on a walk. Listen, and take action. Follow through on your commitment to your relationship. Follow through on your commitment to your goals. Follow through on your commitment to excellence. Follow through on your commitment to your dreams. Follow through on your commitment to your friends and family. Follow through on your commitment to your co-workers and business partners. And most importantly, follow through on your commitment to yourself. What is the worst that can happen?

Chapter Two Wrap-Up: Follow Through

1. What is your own personal definition of success?

2. What is one thing you can follow through on this week?

3. Do you have an example of not following through? What were the consequences?

4. What is a long-term follow-through you would like to see come to fruition?

5. What are the things you need to accomplish that long-term goal?

CHAPTER THREE
ONE, TWO,
THREE...TOGETHER!

"As iron sharpens iron, so one man sharpens another." - Proverbs 27:17

Three weeks after our district finals loss to Hemlock my junior year of high school, we were in a team meeting and already preparing for our senior campaign. We did not want a repeat of our junior year. Our junior year was an utter disappointment. We made a vow that afternoon to make sure we held each other accountable during the spring and summer. Anything less than a state championship was unacceptable.

We wanted to leave behind a legacy that would be remembered forever. Even the underclassmen had bought in. We were mentally at the stage of refining the iron—perfecting by polishing. We knew that to get where we wanted to be next winter, we had to polish up a few things.

Often in our lives, we see refining as a massive change in our daily habits or mental approach when, in fact, small adjustments will benefit us the same or better than big adjustments. Nothing was going to stop us from our goal. We were dedicated to making those small changes. But we were going to lean on each other for assistance. We helped each other that spring. We pushed each other that spring. We challenged each other that spring.

That November, we opened up the 2006–07 basketball season on the road against our league rivals. Our anxiety was at its peak. Part of me believed someone planned that game strategically. The last thing anyone wants is to open the season against their rivals, but it was an opportunity to reveal what we had been refining over the past eight months.

The intensity of the pre-game continued to build as the clock ticked. The clock finally reached "0.0," and it was game time. Both teams got one final word from their head coaches before the tip. Our coach reminded us of what was at stake with this game and told us to have fun and enjoy the moment. Then he said, "Together on three." "ONE, TWO, THREE...TOGETHER," we all yelled.

That mantra spearheaded our entire off-season. We often reflected on the idea of this being our last time playing together. Many of us had been together since middle school, while others joined in high school, but we were all brothers with the love and passion deeper than ever. The expectations were high for this season. We did not want to let our community, our families, or our friends down. But more importantly, we did not want to let each other down. We were in this together, and we had spent the entire off-season refining our skills and our bond as brothers. We were tighter than ever by the end of that summer.

Every sport is a team sport, even if the team members compete as individuals. Track and field athletes need trainers to help them develop based on whether they run long or short events, and they need teammates yelling around the track to give them that extra boost of energy near the finish line. Swimmers need help from trainers with nutrition and from coaches to perfect their technique. Boxers need a team to help them physically and strategically prepare for a fight.

Have you seen *Creed II*? In *Creed II*, Adonis loses the first fight against Drago's son. Then, Rocky takes Adonis into the desert to help him get ready for the next fight. In the desert, Adonis is surrounded by other fighters and their trainers. This is Rocky and Adonis's training team. Adonis would not have been able to defeat Drago's son without the unconventional team in the desert. It was not a natural team setting, but it was his support team at that time.

I learned many irreplaceable lessons being a part of basketball teams. As I got older, I understood how important those lessons were for my character development and growth. I was able to turn those experiences into life models. That is why I decided to write this book about my experiences as an athlete and how they transitioned to my professional career. Important lessons can be learned when you are with a group of brothers or sisters every day grinding after the same goal. Teammates sharpen one another. Teammates hold each other up. Coaches play a vital role in putting together the pieces and making sure they complement one another. If a coach puts together a bad team, there would not be much sharpening or refining.

Being able to collaborate with others is essential in all settings of life. Whether it is a sport setting, volunteer setting, work setting, church setting, or even with your family. A healthy team dynamic is critical. Whether you are struggling in your faith walk, not hitting your goals at work, having trouble with your children or family, struggling with your fitness or health goals, or even marriage, having people around you that you trust can help you get over those hurdles we have in life. Bad relationships and poor teammates will only cause chaos.

When I was little, my brother and I would create massive forts around our living room with sheets and blankets. Building forts was not a one-man task. I am sure you could build forts on your own, but teamwork makes the process efficient. We had to work together to make sure we had the sturdiest forts possible. We were able to develop our problem-solving skills, imagination, social skills, and friendship during that process, which made our bond indestructible. We had a goal, and we were able to see the plan through with each other's help and guidance. We had to rely on each other at certain times during construction of our forts.

Similarly, we need people in our lives that can support and help us. We should not do life alone, and God does not want us to do life alone. That is where the quote "Iron sharpens iron" comes from. We can never truly grasp that concept unless we are willing to be around more iron. Only then can we recognize the knowledge and strength that others bring to the table. Teamwork makes the dream work. Teamwork makes life work.

As adults, we must continue to build on the original foundation of teamwork that we developed working on projects and on teams with our peers. The most important asset to any organization is the people they employ. The organization will flourish as the people within thrive. That is why I encourage student-athletes not to shy away from their athletic experience in job interviews. Characteristics are developed during our time as athletes that can't be duplicated. You have a unique set of skills, and you need to prove how much of an asset you truly are. The hiring manager's job is to find the best fit for the team and the organization.

The hiring process, recruiting process as an athlete, and try-outs are all very similar to one another. The hiring manager and coaching staff are putting together the best team to be successful. Attack interviews the same way you would attack a try-out or a game when you know coaches are in the stands. Attack a business meeting that same way you would attack a scouting report. Attack professional and personal growth the same way you attacked your development as an athlete. Your skills as an athlete are transferable. Do not leave your intensity and passion with the game you love after high school or college. Take those qualities with you and use them to your advantage.

I have always found it ironic as we leave certain chapters of our lives, we often leave behind certain qualities. We grow up, forget about Santa, and lose our imagination. We leave college, spend ten minutes preparing for a job interview, and expect to hear back from the hiring manager. How much time did you spend preparing for competitions? I bet it was more than ten minutes. You are never too old to go back in time to reflect on your past. I like to go back to certain books and reread certain chapters, and we must do the same with our lives. We mature, but never forget to go back to the previous chapters and reflect on what was already written.

To bring together teams and sharpen one another in the professional sector, many organizations adopt team-building activities outside of the normal day-to-day activities. Whether it is taking the team out for drinks or to a ball game, a vital part of ensuring your people are happy is to surround them with people they voluntarily want to be around. Team building helps team members get to know one another outside of the 9-5 grind. Many coaches do the same with their teams. Team building helps with introducing new teammates to their new dynamic and new teammates. This helps to create a family environment amongst teams.

Future Workplace did a study on 10,000 participants spanning over 20 countries. The study concluded that almost two-thirds of the participants said they would be more inclined to stay at their company longer if they had more friends. A separate study, by Officevibe, found that 70% of employees say having friends at work is the most crucial element to a happy working life, and 58% of men would refuse a higher-paying job if it meant not getting along with co-workers. A few years back, I remember my boss taking our team to an escape room in New Orleans. I thought we worked well together in the workplace, but we struggled in the escape room that evening. We came together a little more after that outing. I was still new to the team, but I noticed the positive impact on our communication after the outing.

"Not finance. Not strategy. Not technology. It is teamwork that remains the ultimate competitive advantage, both because it is so powerful and so rare." (Patrick Lencioni, *The Five Dysfunctions of a Team*)

Life is about collaborating with others. This is a skill that is introduced to us at an early age, even if you weren't in sports, and those skills continue to develop over time. When those skills mature, they become the foundation of our character development. Teamwork is a social activity. We develop social skills that will benefit us later in life. We develop a sense of togetherness, allowing us to cultivate relationships. When we develop our social skills at a young age, we begin to develop our abilities to communicate with one another. To be a great team, there has to be good communication. Good communication is a testament to your togetherness as a team. Effective communication is a branch of the trust that has been established. "Research has found that three or more people working together on a project are much more effective than a single person spending all of his time doing the same thing. However, without communication, the three-plus team members can be as useless as if the project went untouched." (Alan Bass)

How can we sharpen others?

- By being a good listener.
- Engaging in difficult conversations.
- Sharing different perspectives with one another.
- Sharing our weaknesses with one another.
- Sharing our heart with one another.

I was watching high school basketball on ESPN one evening, and the player of the game touched on how important the other star players were on their team. The star player communicated how unselfish the team was and how influential that was to his personal growth. The star player noted how he and the other star player competed against each other in practice routinely, and it helped them make each other better. As athletes, we play a pivotal role in helping our teammates get better. When we leave the athletic realm, that responsibility is still ours. Accept it! You are responsible for making your co-workers better. You are responsible for making your workplace better. You are responsible for making your organization better.

And that does not mean only in a leadership position.

You should never keep your passion for making your teammates better away from the world. Encourage your classmate, your younger sister, a friend on the softball team, your graduate assistant helping with the team, the team manager, and even the janitorial staff. You develop skills as an athlete that the world needs. Do not keep your gift and skills to yourself and reserve them only for your past teammates. The world is depending on you to be a light in the darkness.

A very popular debate around the basketball world is who the best duo is in the history of the National Basketball Association. Magic Johnson and Kareeem Abdul-Jabbar, Larry Bird and Kevin McHale, Shaquille O'Neal and Kobe Bryant, and Michael Jordan and Scottie Pippen are often among those suggested. Fans also argue that, without Shaquille O'Neal, Kobe Bryant would not be as successful or, without Kobe Bryant, Shaquille O'Neal would not be as successful. Unfortunately, we will never know the answer to those statements. The fact of the matter is they were together, and they were special together. The duos mentioned above have claimed many NBA championships. Two are better than one. Iron sharpens iron and friends/teammates sharpen each other in the same context. In my eyes, they won championships because of one another, and I know because of the evidence. I can look back at those duos and pull facts about how successful they were as partners.

I have always been intrigued with wolves since I was a kid. A wolf is strongest when it is a part of a pack. Without the support of the pack, a lone wolf has a lower chance of survival. Each wolf in the pack has a unique skill set. Each skill set strengthens the other. "The strength of the pack is the wolf, and the strength of the wolf is the pack." —Rudyard Kipling

The same can be said for us. Our teammates or friends bring a unique personality and skill set to the relationship. At the collegiate level, it is the coaches' job to recruit players that will not only fit in their system but compliment and sharpen one another. In hopes that this would lead to team success. I remember my first basketball recruiting visit. The head coach spoke about how his team was young and needed a leader to get the team going in the right direction. It was not my play on the court that impressed him the most. It was how engaged I was with the game and my teammates while I was resting on the bench. The coach expressed his joy of watching me cheer and lift-up my teammates. That coach was looking to pair my skill set with the current skill set of those already on the team.

I have been a part of positive and negative team dynamics. At some point as former athletes or young workers, it is your responsibility to learn from those experiences and use them for what they are. It is your responsibility to share with a hiring manager those experiences. Whether you were the captain or played a supporting role on your team. You do not need to be a leader to make an impact on your team, campus, or organization. You do not need a job title to be impactful to your organization and community. It is your responsibility to talk about the bad team dynamics you have experienced. How did you overcome the poor team experience? What did you learn about that team? Did you do anything to positively make a difference on the team? Did you step up when your coach called on you to produce? These are all experiences that can be used in real life situations. Do not sell yourself short. Your athletic experience is golden, but you need to make it fit into your life once you depart your respective sport.

God never intended for us to take on life by ourselves. God wants us to have fellowship and grow with one another. In our personal lives, we are the head coach. We are responsible for surrounding ourselves with the right people. There will be battles that we can't spiritually, mentally or physically fight alone. Like the lone wolf, it becomes harder to survive away from the pack. When my grandfather was diagnosed with cancer, he was given a time frame on how long we had with him. I remember the nurse mentioning that my grandfather was still here and fighting due to the outpouring of love from the family. That is how important a strong team is to your survival. It makes fighting easier. Whether you are fighting the number one team in the country or cancer, a great team dynamic will give you a fighting chance.

When iron is used to sharpen iron, heat must be present. The same can be said for the relationships we enter. You cannot sharpen iron when it is cold. Some friends, co-workers, or associates will be able to create that type of warmth in your life. You will have friendships or relationships that do not create any energy and or sharpen you at all. And there is nothing wrong with that. The ones that do not create that warmth only become an issue when they drag you down. Those are the relationships you want to be aware of because you will get comfortable and normalize negative situations with them. You want to make sure you have a stronger line of connection to the people who can reciprocate your warmth and energy.

One bad apple on your team or staff can be detrimental to your growth and success. If you watch sports, you see coaches dismiss players all of the time for not adhering to the team rules. Bad apples have a way of destroying your culture. Bad apples drain your productivity, collaboration, and creativity. Keep that in mind when you are pursuing a new job or a new group of friends in a new city.

The Right Supporting Cast

Casts and splints support and protect injured bones and soft tissue. When you break a bone, your doctor may need to reconstruct the bones and tissue. Casts and splints serve as a mechanism for proper healing. Like the medical use of the term "cast," having a strong supporting cast is essential to your ability to heal properly and get back to full strength on your life journey. A strong and sturdy supporting cast will surround your areas of weakness until the muscular strength is built up in that area of your life. Having the right support in your life will assist in creating a more dynamic team professionally and athletically. Having a strong supporting cast also plays a major role in performance, from athletics to the professional realm.

Like a coach and general manager in professional sports, you are responsible for surrounding yourself with a team of people who will have a positive impact on your life. General managers are responsible for putting a team together that will be successful on the court or field. You must attack life in the same manner.

General managers are not perfect by any means, so do not put too much pressure on yourself for mistakes you make along the way. You can sign someone one day and send them packing the next. We see it all the time in sports. A general manager trades for an athlete and releases that athlete two weeks later. We, on the other hand, have a habit of keeping bad teammates around because it fills a current void. I see it all of the time with friends who are dating. We need to have a general manager mentality when it comes to hiring players. You have to hire people to your team who will encourage you, pick you up, hold you accountable, sharpen you, laugh with you, deliver praise and criticism, and most importantly, be honest with you.

Who is on your advisory board? Business leaders suggest that creating an advisory board is a foundational part of every successful organization. We should stress the same importance in our lives. An advisory board provides advice to business leaders to help them meet their goals. An advisory board is appointed based on their expertise. Advisory board members serve as mentors on our daily walk. Each advisory board member brings something of value to the table. In our lives, it is important that we create an advisory board to help us tackle life and provide advice on topics such as struggles at work, family problems, anxiety, your future, relationships, and life in general. This board can be two individuals or 20. The key is making sure these people are only a call or text away. In business, the last person you want on your board is someone who is just taking up space. You need to recruit individuals who will bring value to the group, not only to benefit you, but to benefit the group. You are the business. Recruit the best people to your personal advisory board.

Having an advisory board for your life gives you two benefits. One, advisory boards deal with disaster relief. Like businesses, we go through times of turmoil and fear. The benefit of having a strong advisory board is knowing you are not alone in the storm. A member on your board may have gone through the same situation. The insight from that member is unmeasurable. We need board members who can talk us off a ledge. Secondly, an advisory board provides you with a bigger network. Now their network becomes your network. I can't emphasize that point enough.

As a young professional, do not burn bridges. Instead, be the star that you are and grow your network. For example, if you lose your job suddenly. This is where having a strong network comes to the rescue. I was recently chatting with a friend about that exact situation. Their industry was crumbling due to COVID-19, and he was released from his position. But thanks to his network, he was in a job shortly after being laid off. When you have a good board, there is a strong possibility you have a strong network. So, it is crucial that you understand that creating your own personal advisory board means you become a call or text away from those on your board members' advisory boards, too.

We only become who God created us to be together. We all need one another. We all need someone to believe in us, cheer for us, and pick us up when needed.

Chapter Three Wrap-Up: One, Two, Three...Together!

1. If iron sharpens iron, who are those people who sharpen you?

2. If you do not have anyone to sharpen you now. How can you fix that? How are you going to find someone to be your iron?

3. What are some influential guidelines you learned from playing team sports? How do you practice those fundamental rules as an adult or a friend outside of your team?

4. Having the right supporting cast is vital to survival. Look through your phone. List five people you can rely on when the game is coming down to the wire.

CHAPTER FOUR
FINISH THROUGH
THE CONTACT

"Life is like any other contact sport. You may encounter hardships of one sort or another. Wise people find happiness not in the absence of such hardships, but in their ability to understand them when they occur." – Sydney Banks

I was never a great one-on-one basketball player. I was never a knock down shooter. I was never really that athletic until I got to college. Therefore, I had to be creative with how I scored baskets. However, I was blessed with long arms, and that played to my benefit on the defensive end. It also helped me slightly on the offensive end. My length helped me get by slower and shorter defenders. I was able to cover a lot of ground very quickly, whether it was from the wing or in transition. This would leave the defender with two decisions: foul me or let me score an easy bucket.

But there are special moments in basketball when there is both a foul and a basket. In the basketball community, we call that an "and one." You can hear players and fans yell those magic words routinely throughout a game. Very few combinations of words create adrenaline like "and one." It is a special combination. Those are the plays I lived for in basketball.

Some sports are more physical than others. And with that physical nature, you must be able to finish through contact—continue toward your goal despite outside influence—of the opposing team. From a soccer player being bumped as they dash down the field to an offensive basketball player attacking the basket, contact is a part of sports.

Finishing a play through the contact of the defender was as exhilarating as my little heart could handle. Finishing through contact of a defender does something to your confidence level as an offensive player. It really is hard to explain the feeling through text in this book. I had a hard time thinking of a feeling that would resonate with readers. I believe it is one of those things you must feel firsthand.

No matter when the "and one" happens in the game, it provides a sense of hope. And what are we without hope in life? In life and in basketball, hope is one of our primary driving forces. Psychologists around the world have studied the many vehicles we need to survive and thrive. Charles Snyder believed that hope was a vehicle that positively impacted how we attacked life and our goals. He developed the Hope Theory. Snyder defined hope as, "A positive cognitive state based on a sense of successful goal-directed determination and planning to meet these goals." In Charles Snyder's Hope Theory, he lists three components for hope:

1. Have focused thoughts.
2. Develop strategies in advance to achieve your goals.
3. Be motivated to make the effort required to reach these goals.

When you focus on positive outcomes, you can develop productive and active strategies to achieve your goals. In turn, you develop a certain type of motivation to help you reach your goals. In basketball terms, I was able to finish through the contact more often when my focus was aligned with positive outcomes. Not being able to finish through the contact can be a symbol of negative thoughts, lack of confidence, negative words from others, memories of past failures, thoughts of generational curses, lack of focus, lack of toughness, and a lack of motivation and courage to finish through the contact.

Finishing through contact served as a mental stimulant for me as a player. And later in my life, those mental stimulants served as victories I could reflect upon. As I mentioned earlier in this chapter, finishing the basket after being fouled is a unique feeling. Some situations require a lot of focus and strength, while others require a certain level of finesse. Finishing through contact away from home as a young adult was difficult for me at the beginning. Like everything we do, it takes practice. When I finished through the contact, I was able to build up hope in my abilities. When I graduated high school, my hope grew in my abilities. When I graduated from college, my hope grew a little more. When I received my first recruitment letter for basketball, my hope grew a little more. When I received my first promotion, my hope grew a little more.

I remember reading a newspaper article around 2013 from back home in Saginaw, Mich. The sheriff from the local police department noted that children in part of the city were growing up in an environment of hopelessness. It hurt to hear a sheriff speak that way about home, but it was true. If the youth in that particular area had a sense of hope, they would strive for a different outcome or possibility. If the parents in the neighborhood had a positive memory to reflect upon relating to finishing through contact, maybe they could get through the day as well. Not only would they get through the day, but they would also be able to pass on that hope to the kids in their home and community. It is hard to develop hope when you do not have any past victories to grasp unto.

Here are a few words that are associated with hopelessness: "uninspired," "powerlessness," and "limitedness." These are all power words that can affect you positively or negatively when trying to finish through the contact we will face in our lives. When you are uninspired, you may buy ice cream after a good workout instead of choosing a healthy option. When you are inspired, you may ask that special guy or girl on a date. When you are powerless, you will struggle navigating through obstacles. When you are powerless, you lack the confidence you need to finish the play or goal. When you are powerless, your pride does not allow you to ask for help. When you are powerless, you lack control.

When the spirit of limitedness takes over, you end up in situations like the sheriff mentioned earlier. When you engage and let limitedness take ahold of your life, you confine yourself to a prison. When limitedness takes control, you see your abilities and circumstances as limited or negative. Your self-talk says, "I can't do that. No one from my family did that. None of my friends did that." When you attack the spirit of limitedness, your self-talk begins to look like this: "I am enough for this world. I can do this. It may take me longer to pass this test, but I will get it done. I am in control." When you conquer the spirit of limitedness, you take control of your future. You "take the bull by the horns."

Usually with limitedness comes labels. When you conquer limitedness, you take control of the labels. "Inspired," "competence," and "limitless" are the positive forms for hope. You can change everything by adjusting your mindset from uninspired to inspired, powerlessness to competence, and limitedness to limitless. It's easier said than done, but with dedication and focus you can shift the negative energy to positive energy. You can do this in many ways. One way could be reading more. Another way could be watching the news less. Another way could be leaving your comfort zone. In any situation, it will take effort.

My mom was a God-fearing woman. As tired as she was at times, she never gave up hope. She never let us see her giving up. After I failed my freshman year of high school, she did not allow the "I'm stupid" label to creep into my mind. She kept pushing me forward.

The game of basketball provided me with hope. It also served as a foundation for me to develop hope in different areas of my life. I was extremely slim during my teenage years, so much so that a close friend during high school called me "Sticks." Because I was so thin, I often thought that everyone saw me as weak. Finishing through contact early in my career was not as easy, but when I was able to finish the play, it gave me confidence and hope. I wasn't as weak as everyone thought. I was strong! I was strong enough physically to finish the play. I was strong enough mentally to finish the play. I focused on the positive outcome and I finished. I knew contact would come, but I absorbed the hit and I finished. That gave me hope!

"And one" may mean more at different times during a game. An "and one" early in the game gave me hope that today was going to be a good day. An "and one" in the fourth quarter could spark a miraculous comeback and propel my team to win, which showed me that when times get tough or when the game is on the line, I can mentally handle the pressure of big moments. It showed me that I could come back after being beat down by labels, anxiety, nerves, depression, or anything else that could negatively impact my spirit and focus. I knew I could finish because I had done it before.

An "and one" symbolizes the ability to get back up after being knocked down. Hope gives us strength to conquer pain and turmoil. Hope gives us strength to be different. Hope gives us strength to push through being uncomfortable for a season.

Three Ways to Finish Through Contact

Expect the Contact

Expecting contact is just a part of the game and should be translated to our daily walk in life. There is a saying, "God never said it would be easy. But he did promise he would never leave us." In that context we must expect contact on our journey the same way I expected contact driving to the basket, the same way a football player expects contact running up the middle of the offensive and defensive lines. Sometimes we fall after contact, and other times a small bump knocks us off course.

And just because we expect contact, does not mean it will not affect us. Contact in life can carry many meanings. We may lose a job, get into an automobile accident, break a bone, fail a physical, lose the starting spot on the team, lose our notes from listening to a speaker, or even losing the paper we had been working on all day. Those are examples of negative contacts that impact our daily walk.

When we expect contact, we prepare ourselves mentally and physically. As a slasher in basketball, I knew there would always be some sort of contact from the defense. That comes with the game of basketball. In basketball, if you don't like contact, you can always play on the perimeter. Unfortunately, life does not work that way. It doesn't matter what you are pursuing— you have to expect contact. You can be an ambitious entrepreneur or a homebody. Life comes with contact. Focus and fight through the contact.

Coaches use certain drills to help their players get comfortable with contact. They prepare their athletes because they know contact will happen eventually. Life is very similar. Contact will come, and if you aren't prepared, it's very likely life will get the better of you. Practice and drills help prepare you. Why don't we have life drills to help us get through contact? The good news is that we *do*. These drills are different for everyone and unique to our circumstances.

Do you squeeze in life drills during your busy day? This could be as simple as using the *5 Second Rule* from Mel Robbins or as complex to managing your finances weekly on a Microsoft Excel spreadsheet. Are you putting a certain amount of money into your savings or investment app each week? Did you create a plan to be successful your first 90 days on your new job? Did you make an effort to meet everyone on the staff to find out what their role is with the organization? Did you meal prep on the weekend to stay on track with your health goals? Do you meditate daily for stress management? Do you turn off the television at a certain time each night to spend time writing in your journal? What are you listening to on your way to class or work? Are you feeding your mind and spirit positive energy in the morning? Are you spending 30 minutes being active to stay on pace with your fitness goals? Are you reading daily? Are you stepping out of your comfort zone to network with new faces in your new city? This is one of my favorite ones. Everyone wants to leave their hometown until they get their first taste of contact. It is at that moment most people forfeit their goals. How are you preparing for pain? How are you preparing for the contact of betrayal? What drills do you find most effective in helping you finish through the contact of life?

It is naive to go through life without practice. Most coaches show up to practice with a list of items they plan to accomplish that day. It's almost irresponsible if we go through life without our own individual daily practice plan preparing us for finishing through contact. Practice does not mean you will score every bucket when confronted with contact. But you have a higher chance of an "and one" if you have the strength and focus to get the ball near the basket. Practice also does not mean the referees will actually call the foul during the game. A coach once told our team, "Don't leave the game in the

side of the highway once in Kentucky just to worship and stay in the moment with him. Every moment I could meet him, I did!

I am sure without practicing that the past five years, I would have struggled in that area during the COVID-19 pandemic. But I was used to meeting God outside of the church building. So, when churches closed their doors, it was business as usual for me. Now that is only one area of life of course, but we all have different situations when it comes to finishing through contact. I was able to finish through the contact of the physical church being closed. If I had not practiced for that area of my life, I am sure I would have struggled with everyone else.

Not only did I expect the contact, I prepared for the contact. *Expecting* the contact can only take you so far. You need to *prepare* for the contact. When I was a kid, I expected to get a spanking after doing something bad at school. So, what did I do when I got home? I prepared for the spanking by loading up on underwear. Through mental and physical preparation, you can combat the tough times as well. Preparation isn't pain proof, but it will aid in lessening the welts on your bottom.

As you master your practice techniques, you become stronger, and you increase your ability to finish through the contact.

Focus your Thoughts

Dr. Wayne Dyer states, "Every thought impacts you. Every thought has the ability to strengthen you or weaken you." You may be familiar with the saying, "Your words can be life or death." The same can be said for our individual thoughts. Our thoughts have the ability to create life-giving energy or destructive energy. Stay conscious of what you are thinking at all times. Thoughts are the foundation of Charles Snyder's Hope Theory. Dr. Dyer believes we are made up of how we see the world. Our perspective plays a vital role in how we see the world and how we decipher it.

Focusing your thoughts on positive outcomes is important when you are trying to finish through the contact. If you believe you can't finish through the contact, you won't. If you believe you aren't smart enough to obtain a master's degree, you won't. If you believe you can't run a marathon, you won't. If you believe you can't fast for 24 hours, you won't. If you believe you can't open that coffee stand, you won't. If you believe the world is out to get you, it will.

According to studies, positive thoughts and positive thinking play an enormous role in our personal health and stress management abilities. The journey of creating this positive and productive culture starts from within. As Dr. Dyer suggested, our thoughts have the ability to build us up and make us strong or weaken us. In layman terms, negative thoughts are pretty much our kryptonite.

Like everything I have talked about in this chapter. Practice is crucial. It takes practice and devotion to feed our mind positive images. I am writing this book in 2020, and that statement couldn't mean more. Social media is a feeding frenzy for negative images and conversations, but because we are so reliant on social media for many reasons we do not see it as a problem. That is why it is important to fast from social media like many fast from food. I am not the best at fasting from eating, but when I do fast, I usually fast from things like social media and working out.

We live in a world full of information, and it is hard to decipher what is true and false. That noise creates division amongst us as humans. That same noise can create a division in our minds, which leads to a diversion in our minds. The noise continually feeds our mind, and we build our perspective of what we see or hear. If all we see is fire around us, that is how we will see the world we live in.

Try to feed your mind and spirit positive information in the morning—as soon as you get up. I find it extremely hard to create positive energy around my life if the first thing I do in the morning is turn on the news and surround my thoughts with fire. I can't start my day off on the right foot if I get in my car and feed my ears negative music. I love hip-hop. I grew up on hip-hop, but it does not have the same effect as it once did. I still need it for days when I am in the weight room but those are different situations. I personally can't feed my mind hip-hop before noon.

using my guard arm better. It wasn't long before I adjusted my approach. These weren't massive adjustments, but they were massive in regards to their effectiveness on the court. The small adjustments helped me finish at the rim at a higher efficiency. Then, there were the rim protectors.

Just like a video game, as the levels went on, the harder they became. As we got older, the competition advanced, too. Rim protectors were no longer 6'3, they were 6'10. The athletes were jumping higher and were able to recover faster on defense. The underhand layup was not as effective as it was before. So, I had to change that as well. I had to learn to turn the ball over. Either I had to float it high enough for the rim protector to miss it or dunk the ball to keep my opponent from pinning it on the glass. I had to make these changes to give myself a chance to finish through the contact. We have to give ourselves a chance to finish through the contact and that means making small adjustments when they are necessary. I repeat, SMALL!

We need to make the proper adjustments as we go through life. Praying once a day may have worked in the previous season, but it does not mean it will work ten years down the line. Life advances much like the game of basketball. Jobs advance as you move up the ranks. What you did as an entry-level worker may not work at the next level. How you think at the entry-level will not be how you need to think at the senior level. The game changes. Life changes.

I had to make small adjustments to protect the ball better. You will need to make the appropriate adjustments to protect areas you value in your life. Protect your heart. Protect your thoughts. Protect your spirit. Protect your eyes. Protect your mind. Protect your ears. Defenders will be looking to strip you of the ball on your way to the basket. Opposition will be looking to strip you of your spirit on your walk. Defenders will be looking to strip you of your joy. Naysayers will be looking to strip you of your passion. Defenders will be looking to strip you of your dreams. Defenders will be looking to strip you of your peace. Defenders will be looking to strip you of your optimism. Protect the ball!

Chapter Four Wrap-Up: Finish Through the Contact

1. How often do you focus on positive outcomes?

2. Do you hang around people who focus on the negative? Are these people a part of your support cast?

3. Write down one goal you would like to accomplish this month. How are you going to keep your focus on this goal? What kind of strategies would help you keep focus? How will you stay motivated? (Ex: Are you going to communicate with your supporting cast more? Are you going to stay away from negative energy? Are you going to focus your thoughts on the outcome? Are you going to start your morning with positive thoughts?

4. Reaching your goal this month will not be easy. What life drills can you incorporate daily or weekly to help you accomplish your goal(s)?

CHAPTER FIVE
FINISH THROUGH
THE LINE

"Resistance is greatest just before the finish line." - Anonymous

I didn't play many sports growing up, but I assume finishing through the line is common lingo amongst many sports in some respect. In track and field, you physically must cross the line to complete the race. In football, coaches stress the importance of finishing through the line during drills or sprints. A Division I track and field video surfaced of a runner prematurely celebrating and being passed right at the finish line. Unfortunately, that is a tough way to learn the lesson of finishing through the line.

I have been that runner at certain times in my life. Sometimes a punch in the gut can be the best learning experience. It is not the best feeling, but it is a lesson that can be used to motivate us in the future. In the previous chapter, I mentioned using past positive experiences to aid in pushing you through tough times. You can also use experiences that resulted in a negative outcome.

Growing up playing basketball, finishing through the line was the difference between one more sprint at the end of practice —that was the result if one of my the teammates failed to cross the line before the clock struck zero— and going home for the night.

Why do coaches emphasize finishing through the line? It seems like an obvious concept. Why wouldn't you want to finish as fast as possible? Why do we naturally want to slow down or stop right before the finish line? Why are we wired that way? Why are there so many videos of football players dropping the ball right before crossing the goal line?

Runners have a leg up on most of us when it comes to developing the mentality of pushing through the finish line. They are trained to cross the finish line strong. They spend their entire lives pushing through the line with the support of their team, coaches, and loved ones. Like many aspects of the sports realms, I believe there are life principles in the act of pushing yourself beyond the finish line. It is more than a form of punishment. It is a life analogy. How often did you get to the end of an assignment and slack off? When was the last time you had to meet a deadline for a project and eased up toward the end? When was the last time you were in the gym and skipped one more rep even though you know you could have pushed out one more?

I want to spend time connecting the dots about the finish line and life. How are they similar? How did that concept shape me as an adult? Why did my coaches emphasize this so much? Was it punishment or was it more? When I started planning the layout of this book. I reflected on a time I did a mock interview with a senior recruiter early on in my career. The senior recruiter applauded my interview skills. I was not a professional with ten years of experience. I was interviewing for an entry-level position with little experience in the field. I was able to tailor their job description to my experience as an athlete. I wanted to share my story and reflect on how I made sense of my journey as an athlete and professional. I realized they all seemed to connect in some way. My experiences shaped me into who I am.

We all have unique experiences that shape us. Working in intercollegiate athletics, I would hear stories of athletes struggling to transition to life after competition. Then I wondered, "What about all the high school kids who don't get the opportunity to play the game they love? How are they managing the transition?"

As I grew professionally, I started to see the connections between sports and life. I realized the grind was still the same. I was on a team, and we wanted to be successful. Every job I held, I needed to meet a goal individually and with my team. If you do a decent job in your position, sometimes you get recruited by other organizations. It was just like being a basketball prospect again. Sure, I wasn't throwing no look passes anymore. No look passes took a different form in the professional realm. Maybe the no look pass was bringing donuts to the office. Maybe it was throwing a lead to a co-worker if they were having a bad week or month. Maybe, it was stopping to see a season ticket holder randomly to spark a connection. Maybe, it was bringing pizza for my students while they were fundraising on the phones.

I originally saw finishing through the line as a punishment. As an adult, I see it as creating a good habit, a way to protect your focus, or a way to build grit. I see finishing through the line as a way of making sure I always push through, no matter how I tired I am. It's a way to build character and build champions. I see finishing through the line as a way to fix our eyes past the finish line.

Finishing through the line matters! Whether you are trying to finish a new diet, a "new year, new you" workout plan, your senior year of college, or a new book. "Finish through the line" is a phrase I carry with me daily. Change the perspective. Instead of viewing it as a punishment, look at it as a mantra, and recite it daily.

1. Finishing through the line develops your self-discipline.
2. Finishing through the line creates a foundation for developing good habits.
3. Finishing through the line develops self-discipline.

Continually stopping short of the finish line creates massive implications. Think back to the story earlier in this chapter. The collegiate runner slowed down and started to celebrate before crossing the finish line. The runner ended up losing the race in the conference tournament. We take a significant risk when we stop short of the finish line or celebrate prematurely.

We display a lack of discipline when we stop short of the finish line. To accomplish anything, you must have discipline. Are you doing what is necessary to be better? Are you following your words with the appropriate actions necessary to accomplish your goals? Disciplining your thoughts also plays a vital role in your success. If you are constantly feeding your mind bad images, you will create a bad energy field. Feed your mind positive thoughts and energy routinely.

I would battle with myself routinely while writing this book. Some days I would forego writing to go fish. Now, fishing isn't a bad habit, but it got in the way of my writing. That is why self-discipline is vital to finishing through the line. You are at war daily with yourself. When I would have a bad thought, I would try to immediately pray or meditate to combat the negative thought. But I can't fight that battle without the proper discipline. Bobby Knight once said, "Discipline: doing what you have to do, and doing it as well as you possibly can, and doing it that way all the time."

Not finishing through the line can impact those around you negatively as well. When we walk or jog through the line, we give reasons for others to follow suit. It can be bad for your team, your professional organization, your family, and even friends. Someone is always watching you from a distance. Some people are watching you to promote you to a higher position. Some people are watching you to figure out how to change their lives. If they see you not pushing through the finish line, they will assume that pushing themselves is not necessary.

Leaders who see you jogging through the line will move on to a different recruit to bring on their team. In a team atmosphere, that energy spreads like a wildfire. The last thing you want is to pass on your lackluster energy. It's just as easy to spread negative energy as it is to spread positive energy. Why do you think the news has such high ratings? I am not saying watching the news is a bad thing but consider the impact of digesting the news first thing in the morning every day.

You cheat yourself when you slow up at the finish line. It's funny how we can become so upset with others when they cheat us, but we don't show the same enthusiasm when we cheat ourselves. We shrug it off and move on. We have one more gear we can tap into, but we often don't because we are comfortable with jogging or walking through the line. That is why I believe finishing through the line matters so much to coaches. Growth is at the end of pushing ourselves beyond what we physically can do. How would we ever know how much we can handle if we never push ourselves beyond what we physically think we can do?

Self-discipline makes us mentally and physically stronger. Self-discipline has many definitions. The definition I prefer is, "The ability to avoid unhealthy excess of anything that could lead to negative consequences." Discipline is essential in every area of our lives. From getting up when your alarm goes off to going to sleep at a reasonable time. Discipline is setting your alarm and not hitting snooze five times before you get out of bed. It takes patience and dedication to build up our discipline muscle. Establishing discipline is not an overnight fix.

When your self-discipline is strong, you can stay true to your word and goals. You are able to hold yourself accountable without the help of others. Making decisions is tough. Following through on those decision is even tougher. When we follow through, though, we strengthen our discipline muscle.

When I first started drinking herbal tea at night, it was extremely easy. It was a fresh goal of mine to partner with my reading habits. Whenever I would read, I would steep some tea right before reading. But after a while, the eagerness dwindled. I would just dive right into my book before prepping any tea. My willingness to follow through was not as strong anymore. My self-discipline was still strong in the area of reading, but I became less interested in the tea. That is where discipline comes in to play. You can grow your discipline in a multitude of ways, but small actions to me are the most important in building discipline. The small actions matter the most. Small actions grow into habits. So, I had to come up with a new plan. I would heat the water before I showered, and I would let the tea steep during that time. Coaches must make small adjustments during the game if they want to win. We must make small adjustments on our daily walk if we plan to follow through on our goals. You are probably thinking, "That's too much pressure to put on myself." But it's not! When you make a decision, it's your responsibility to follow through on that decision.

Like basketball, it's the little things in life that matter the most, like the extra effort of hedging a ball screen in basketball. A hedge in basketball takes place when a defender guarding a player without the ball slides out aggressively to stop the ball handler from a clear path to the basket. This small detail allows his teammate to recover after being screened. Something so small can mean so much in a tight game. Maybe the ball handler turns the ball over, or you force the guard to be out of his shooting range. The little things matter in basketball and life. Steeping the tea while I showered was a small action and didn't require much.

Self-discipline is easier said than done, though. We live in a busy world where we must have the discipline to choose between spending massive hours on our phones scrolling social media or spending quality time with loved ones. It is hard to find time to remain disciplined. (I say that as I am writing the end of this chapter on my smartphone.)

Make life work for you. There will never be a perfect time to lose weight. There will never be a perfect time to go back to school. There will never be a perfect time to quit your job and open your own consulting business. Or any number of other dreams you may have! You may be thinking, "I hear you Andrew, but how do I get better in that area of my life?" Here is my answer: Focus on the little things. Take baby steps towards what you are trying to accomplish.

I have wanted to write a book for almost six years now. Year after year, I put it off. In 2015, I sat back and put together a plan to start the process. I started using social media to post my thoughts more. Those posts turned into articles that I would write. Then I made a personal website and started blogging. Then two years ago, I finally started writing. It all started with baby steps. What you will build taking small steps is confidence. Your confidence will grow and your inner strength will grow. Self-discipline is about self. To help yourself, you must have faith in yourself. Small steps will help you grow that faith in yourself.

Foundation of Good Habits

Joyce Meyer said in her book *Making Good Habits, Breaking Bad Habits*, "Don't wait to 'feel' like doing a thing to do it. Live by decision, not emotion." Finishing through the line is a decision. Following up on a meeting with a mentor is a decision. Asking a girl on a date is a decision. Waking up at 6:30am to get to the gym is a decision. Setting your alarm ten minutes earlier to pray is a decision. Fasting from social media is a decision. Staying in the weight room for 20 more minutes after having a sluggish workout is a decision. Sitting in a room full of people and talking about tough topics is a decision.

Creating positive habits is ultimately a decision because our brains cannot decipher a good habit from a bad habit. The brain will just receive whatever we decide to incorporate in our lives, whether those habits are good or bad. Once the habit is established, it is hard to change it up. When my grandmother passed a few years back, after the funeral, I went to the weight room. That is how I dealt with life at that point as an adult. I developed a habit of being in the gym to get through my day. I had been alone and traveling for quite a while at that point in my life. I didn't have family or friends around much during that time. The habit was created and engrained in my mind. I left my family at my parent's house and released my grief in the best way I knew how. My family probably thought I was crazy, but that was the healthy habit I had created to deal with life. Lifting was more than a physical activity, it had become a mental activity. I can't tell you how many times I have cried in a gym over the past five years. That day was no different.

It takes discipline to create good habits. That is why finishing through the line has always been important to every coach across the globe. Though it can be used for physical conditioning, it plays a huge role in mental conditioning. Finishing through the line is all about creating a positive habit to have in your back pocket. You will develop a ton of bad habits on this life journey. It is essential that you have a few good ones for when you really need them. Take the story above about my grandmother's death. The weight room was my place of grief and comfort.

You may be asking yourself, "How do I deal with the bad habit that has been corrupting my life for the past ten years?" I could put a list of ten ways to help you create good habits, but you only need one to get the ball rolling. Finish through the line! This is a very small task.

What is one small decision you can make tomorrow to break a bad habit? Is it waking up two minutes earlier? Is it inviting someone to lunch? Is it smiling or waving at a random person? Is it passing on a compliment to someone? Is it sharing a story with someone younger? Is it giving someone a fist bump when you walk past them? Is it bringing donuts to the office? Is it putting on a tie once a week? Is it sending a text to one person a month to just say "thank you"? Is it brushing your teeth after lunch? Is it saying, "good morning"? That may be an obvious one, but you would be surprised by how many people don't take the time to say "good morning" when they cross paths with another human. You may also ask yourself, "How do I maintain that good habit?" Well, I hate to repeat myself but *finish through the line*!

Don't get so lost in steps that you forget to create the actual habit you want to change. It starts with making a small decision to finish through the line. Breaking bad habits is no easy task. We judge which habits are good and bad for us. Basketball is a game of habits. Life is a game of habits. Like basketball, we can read every instruction book known to mankind. But change will never come until we practice what we read.

Pushing yourself through the finish line can be tough and mentally exhausting. The coach serves as the accountability partner in basketball. Would athletes sprint through the line themselves without the coach breathing down their backs? Would we push through one more set on the squat rack without the support of our trainer? Would we skip going to Whataburger for dinner after a great workout without some form of accountability? Would we pursue our dreams without that friend constantly asking us about it? Probably not at the start. But we create that accountability and habit the more we practice finishing through the line. Having someone who can be your accountability partner is essential in this process. It's awesome when we can physically and mentally get ourselves over the hump, but that is not always possible. Having the right person on your left, your right, or behind you is crucial to getting you through the finish line.

During the 2019–20 collegiate basketball season, a photo started circulating of a point guard lifting up his center's head as they walked back down the court. We are only human. We need friends and family who will pick us up after we make mistakes. Our minds will play tricks on us when we try to attack life by ourselves. "You are not good enough to do this." "You are not strong enough to do that." "You do not have enough willpower to accomplish that." The game of life is easier with those supporting team members around us. Life isn't an individual sport.

It is important that I leave you with this thought: The finish line has always been recognized as the end of the journey. I like to see the finish line as the start to a new day, which is why finishing through the line is so important. We need momentum to push through tough times. We need momentum to achieve our goals. If you get to the end of week one of a diet and start to relax, it will only make week two that much harder. When you have a great week in sales and you get to Friday and relax, you are planning to go into week two with no momentum. Momentum is a very powerful tool, and it should not be carried lightly. We have an opportunity to push ourselves past the finish line. Not because it is the end, but because it is only the beginning. Finish through the line!

Chapter Five Wrap-Up: Finish through The Line

1. What are a couple good habits you would like to instill in your daily walk?

2. What does "self-discipline" mean to you?

3. What area of your life could use a little more confidence?

4. The finish line is the start of a new beginning. Do you have a goal to accomplish after you finish your one-month goal from chapter four? How are you going to keep the momentum into the following month? (Ex: Transition from one month to the next. Transition from one goal to the next.)

CHAPTER SIX
FIGHT THROUGH
THE SCREEN

"Never neglect the little things. Never skimp on that extra effort, that additional few minutes, that soft word of praise or thanks, that delivery of the very best that you can do. It does not matter what others think. It is of prime importance, however, what you think about you. You can never do your best, which should always be your trademark, if you are cutting corners and shirking responsibilities. You are special. Act it. Never neglect the little things." - OG Mandino

Ball screens are essential to any offensive scheme in the game of basketball. A ball screen is an offensive basketball play in which a non-ball-handling offensive player screens a defender by placing their body between the defender and a teammate. The offensive player is able to use the screen to create options for himself and his teammates. Every coach has to find creative ways to get their players in the best position to score. Ball screens happen to be one of the most effective ways to create scoring opportunities. Fighting or getting through a ball screen is essential in playing good individual and team defense. It is also essential if you plan on staying on the court throughout the course of a game. If you are weak defending screens, there is a good chance you will be sitting next to the coaching staff most of the game.

A ball screen in basketball can be defended in many ways, but the main focus here is about fighting through the screen and using proper communication. If you want to learn more about defending ball screens, the internet will be your best friend on your hunt for ball screen knowledge. There is no shortage of professionals who would love to break down every way to defend the ball screen.

As a teammate, you are responsible for helping your team be successful. When a basketball player allows themselves to be screened without a fight, they are putting their team at a disadvantage. They are also showing their teammates that it is alright to go out there and do the same. When you are not the one getting screened, you are responsible for helping your teammate by communicating where the screen is coming from. Fighting through a ball screen is not fun. Fighting through a ball screen is a task no one necessarily enjoys doing. It requires more energy and effort from the on-ball defender.

Kanye West once said in a popular song, "To me, giving up is way harder than trying." That is the mentality players need when fighting through ball screens. That is the mentality many athletes carry with them daily while they grind. Sure, some days may be easier than others, but that mentality helps them push through. Your competitive mentality should not be left behind when you stop competing in your respective sport. Whether you are looking to go pre-med or start your own non-profit, your competitive nature made you a superior athlete in high school or college and will assist you in your professional endeavors. Your competitive mentality is exactly why many organizations recruit former athletes. Your athletic mentality is what you need to make a long-distance relationship work. Your athletic mentality is what you need when a pandemic rocks your world and you lose your job. Your athletic mentality is what you need when it feels like the walls are closing in on you. Your athletic mentality is what you need when you are looking to attack your diet goals, when friends tell you your dream is too big, or when you want to go deeper on your faith journey. Your athletic mentality is what you need when you are on your third attempt to pass the GRE. Your athletic mentality is what you need when you are metaphorically fighting through the ball screens of life.

I wish I could say I was never hit by a blind ball screen. If you watch basketball, you have seen it happen, or maybe you have been on the wrong side of a blind ball screen. If you are or were a guard, you have been associated with a blind ball screen at least once during your life. It is not a good feeling. Blind life ball screens are equally scary. I wish I could say that life will not hit you with a few blind ball screens, but that is not how life works. Some life ball screens will put you down for a while, very similar to being hit by a 250-pound forward or center, while others you will be able to rebound from quickly.

Fighting through ball screens is not for the faint of heart. The Youngstown State University football team carried a "grit" theme during their 2019 football season. Grit—courage in the face of difficulty—is what you need when fighting through screens in basketball and the ball screens of life. Grit is what you need after being hit by a blind ball screen. Fighting through the ball screen takes extra effort from the defender. Those who are not willing to give that extra effort will not be successful. At that point, you will be looked at as a liability.

At a basketball game, you will most likely hear a loud horn following someone not fighting through the screen. This horn symbolizes a sub coming off the bench, and it is one of those rare occasions when you don't necessarily know why the coach took out the player. But those of us who have been around basketball know why they are sitting on the bench now.

Like in sports, you are easily replaceable in the professional realm. Someone is always looking to take your spot. Your goals and dreams will be pursued and accomplished by someone willing to put in the extra effort. I am not ashamed to say that I am one of those people. I was always the underdog in everything. I was never the smartest or most talented. Which meant, I had to work harder than others. I had to work harder at studying in college. I had to put in more time in the gym to get better. It was very difficult for me to gain weight, which meant I had to put in more work in the weight room. I now know I can accomplish what I set my heart on with extra effort. Maybe I don't have to work as hard anymore as a professional, but that is the thing about creating habits—they don't go away very easily. There is no turning it off for me now. It's who I am!

In a previous chapter, I talked about doing small things to change or maintain good habits. Those small things are you applying extra effort. Buying a planner is a small extra effort step. Once you buy the planner, you must practice entry into the planner. Extra effort does not have to be a massive change. I think many people associate extra effort with driving across the country to save a forest or something. That is not the case. Extra effort is just that: extra! Extra effort is sending your brother and sister a good morning text every now and again to stay in touch. That literally takes two seconds to do. That is not a big move, but it is a move nonetheless. Extra effort is anything extra from your ordinary routine. It truly means more energy and effort than you usually put out or into something.

I wanted to pray and meditate more often during my day. I had to come up with a plan. I am away from home 12 hours a day. When I get home, I have to cook and get ready for bed. Then once I get in bed, I like to grab the book on my nightstand and read. By the time I am done reading, the last thing on my mind is prayer or meditation. I asked myself, how can I squeeze in more mediation? So, I started waking up ten minutes earlier in the morning. I spent those ten minutes praying and meditating. Some days it is nine minutes. Some days it is only five minutes. It's all extra for me—a little extra effort that paid dividends for my mental and spiritual health.

For 2 ½ years, I abstained from sex. There were countless times I felt like giving up. The conversations I had with God were pure comedy as I reflect on that time of my life. I wish I could go back and listen to those conversations I would have with him in that studio apartment in Louisiana. "Come on, bruh! You need to get her away from me. . . like now!" How am I going to get through the night? How am I going to get through the week? How am I going to get through the month? I had to make small adjustments.

It was the extra effort in some areas of my life. I had to cut down on my alcohol consumption. Instead of working out for one hour, I would go two hours on the tough days. Then I realized the more time I spent in the gym, the more images I was susceptible to. I had to see other images while working out. This meant I needed to not only work my physical muscles while training, but I also needed to work my mental muscles. The disruptive visual images and thoughts were one of those life blind ball screens. I was getting blasted at times! That is why my life group was so important during that time. I had my guys helping me defend against that particular screen.

It was not easy, but neither is fighting through a screen in a game. It never gets easy but fighting helps you get through it. Having teammates call out the screens plays a huge role in defending the screen effectively. Having life teammates will help you defend the screens during your daily walk.

What kind of screens are you getting hit with currently? What are you trying to accomplish? Are you trying to start a blog? Spend time visualizing your blog's appearance, or join a writing group. Are you trying to lose weight? Visualize standing on the scale and seeing yourself down ten pounds. Join a gym filled with positive people who will keep you motivated. Do you want to own your own boutique? Visualize the ribbon cutting for your business. Network with other business owners or business loan officers. Are you looking for a new career? Start being proactive in your search. Take responsibility for what you are feeling. Build relationships with other professionals. Pick their brain about their daily activities in their role. Be intentional about your conversations. Ask people close to you, "What kind of profession do you see me in?" People who know you will have great insight for you.

When I shifted to a new role recently on campus, a close associate mentioned that he couldn't see me being an athletic director. Some may read this and say, "You can't let that person be negative and kill your spirit." But it is your responsibility to have people around you who can help you along the way, whether it is positive or negative. The worst thing you can do is have associates who will never go against the grain with you. I didn't see his comments negatively. It was a genuine observation, and it really helped me see my career change in a different light. I saw him as a man who had been around these types of professionals most of his adult life. He was able to grasp the personal attributes for the job and what it took to be successful. I would be stupid to not receive his feedback. At that moment, I was excited about the career shift.

One afternoon, I was checking out at Big Lots in Boardman, Ohio. The lady in front of me was purchasing some big storage totes. She was shopping alone and asked the cashier, "Can I leave these here while I drop off the others at my car?" The cashier of course obliged. A young man who also worked at Big Lots approached the cashier soon after and asked, "Do I need to put these back on the shelf?" The cashier told him, "No, a lady bought those, and she will be back in to pick them up." The young man immediately picked up the storage totes and carried them to the lady's car.

I intentionally watched him take the totes to her car so I could see her reaction. The lady was so appreciative of his customer service and support. She was smiling from ear to ear from the small gesture. Something so simple. Something so small. Just a little extra effort. He wasn't *required* to do that. I walked over to the young man and said, "Don't ever stop doing the little things and putting in the extra effort. Even something that small."

A similar situation happened when I worked at Meijer during college. It was a sunny summer afternoon, and I had clocked out and was heading to my car after my shift. A mom had just loaded up the kids and put all the groceries in her truck. As I was walking past her, I told her I would take the cart for her. I am not sure why I did it. It honestly was just second nature. But what transpired after is another sign of what kind of energy can come from doing the little things.

One of my co-workers saw what I did. I wasn't intentionally looking to attract her attention. Later in our lives, as our friendship developed, she told me that she knew I was different when I put that lady's cart back. She was sitting in her car for her break when it happened. I had wondered why all of a sudden, she was so friendly at work! It was a little extra effort that intrigued her. It was something so small and irrelevant in my eyes, but it was something meaningful and valuable to another. That small gesture hinted to someone from the opposite sex that I could be a potential mate.

You must understand the implications that will follow when others see you not fighting through ball screens. Understand how it looks when you don't put in the extra effort needed to be successful on the defensive end. Understand the implications of mentees watching you not put in the extra effort on your job. It's very similar to a basketball game. When you don't fight through screens in life, you are putting your family and friends at a disadvantage. A CEO once told me, "People are always watching you," . . . whether you believe they are or not. Know that they are and that you are responsible for what they see.

You have a responsibility to leave the game better than you found it. You have a responsibility to create a culture at your school. You have a responsibility to show them there is another way. You have a responsibility to break generational curses on your family.

Underclassman are taking notes on how to play the game the right way. Back home, we often argue about who the best team was to come out of Bridgeport High School. Of course, the class of 2007 has a strong argument for being the best team ever. And we mainly argue with the team that made it to the final four in 2009. We lost one game prior to the final four of the state tournament. Not only did we lose, we got destroyed. So, it is usually a hard argument when we talk about the best team ever. I always argue that, yes, the 2009 team made it to the Breslin Center where the state of Michigan hosts the final four teams of the state tournament, but how did they leave the program? The class of

2007 could be considered the best team ever because most of the guys who were on our team were also on that final four team in 2009. Would they have made it to the Breslin Center without that experience with us? No one will ever know. As talented as they were, they were able to fight through the screens with us in 2007, which gave them the experience they could take to the next season and the season after that. So, I will always say we were the best team ever because of how we left the program.

Below are a coach's three rules for fighting through a screen:

1. Be willing to do whatever it takes to get through the screen.
2. No excuses.
3. Every exchange isn't going to be pretty, but if you are willing to fight, you can still get the job done.

Those are three great rules to consider as we fight through screens in life. On this journey, you will get hit with hard screens that knock you down and some weak screens that you can easily fight through. Having great teammates around you will help you defend screens. Extra effort will keep you in the game. Grit will help you fight through screens. Grit will help you get back up after being knocked down.

Chapter Six Wrap-Up: Fight through The Screen

1. Who are your life teammates?

2. Can you count on them to communicate with you and give you a hand after being knocked down?

3. Who would you trust to give you a straight answer about you professional status?

4. What screens have you been hit with lately?

5. What area requires extra effort in your life?

6. What is your plan to maintain that extra effort in the future?

CHAPTER SEVEN
ONE MORE!

"Being part of a team that was so unselfish was amazing. What we were able to accomplish was very meaningful, and what we were able to get done as a team." - Bart Starr

While attending a basketball game or practice, you may hear players scream, "One more!" This usually signifies your teammate to pass the ball around the perimeter one more time to another teammate. The game moves so fast, and sometimes players don't notice the teammate to the left or right of them. Communication from your teammates is vital in this scenario. The ball handler is trusting their teammates' communication and trusting the teammate to knock down the open shot. The shot may not always go in, but the trust is there, the communication is there, and that is what matters.

That is why it is important that you check up on your close friends and family. Life moves so fast that we can lose track of where everyone is located in life. When we yelled, "One more!" on the court, it was a signal that I was right beside you. If the defense was trying to recover, the extra pass may be to a wide-open teammate for a higher percentage shot. One more pass in life can help someone off the ledge. One more pass in life can be a shoulder to cry on. One more pass in life can be you sharing your struggles with someone you trust. One more pass in life can be a friend texting you with a prayer request. One more pass in life can be an invite to a life group.

A study was presented at the Sports Analytic Conference. The researchers had discovered that, "when a defender is more than 6 feet away, the shooting percentage is 40%." That is a staggering number when you are a coach and preaching to your team to be unselfish and make the extra pass. Sure, the "one more" drill is meant to help develop teamwork among the team members, but the numbers don't lie. It boils down to this question, "Do you want to score more points?" The object of any competition is to beat the other team. Defeating the competition is extremely difficult. So why not increase your odds by understanding the facts. Open shots are easier to make than contested shots.

Many teams practice this to develop an unselfish mentality among the team members, but it also yields a higher field goal percentage for a few reasons:

1. The defense is usually scrambling due to a breakdown.
2. An open shot is always better than a contested shot.
3. Basketball is a game of rhythm, and that extra pass is a natural part of that rhythm during a game.

Coach Bryce Drew said, "Many times, one more pass can be the difference between a good shot and a great shot." I will take it a step further and say, one more pass can be the difference between a win or a loss, a championship or second place. One more pass means everything! Being unselfish at the right moment is everything. There are times when being selfish is necessary, and then there are times when being unselfish yields a better result. And that is for life in general.

Making the right pass at the right time can also swing the momentum during the game. As a guard, I understand how a great assist can shift the direction of a game in a blink of an eye. An assist in basketball is when a player distributes the ball to a teammate, which results in a field goal. The player passing is awarded with the assist and the player receiving the pass is awarded with the field goal. A great assist has the ability to elevate the fans, the coach, your teammate, and the team overall.

As a guard, my favorite of those was the ability to lift my teammate. There is no better feeling than encouraging and feeding a teammate who then knocks down a shot or dunks an alley-oop. It gets your teammates involved in the game and builds their confidence. A great assist in life can have a similar impact. A great assist in life can help a friend finish graduate school. A great assist in life can help a single mom make it through another month financially and mentally. A great assist in life can help a friend beat addiction. A great assist in life can provide a friend with a smile. A great assist in life can help a friend trust again, make the right decision, or boost their confidence. A great assist in life can comfort a friend during a tough time, lift their spirit, or even change their life.

Basketball is a team sport, and so is life. We need people. We need small groups in the church to encourage us on our walk. We need people to lift us up when we stumble. We need people who will throw us an alley-oop on a break to rejuvenate our spirit. We need people to hold us accountable. We need people to communicate with us when we aren't seeing things as clearly as we should because life is moving so fast. An assist is essential in basketball, and it is extremely essential on our daily walk.

The Fundamentals of Passing

In many sports, being able to pass is essential to the success of the team. I remember playing with my nephews and nieces when they were toddlers and instructing them to pass me the ball. I remember those moments because they meant everything to me growing up. I look back at it now, and I was responsible for helping them understand the concept of being unselfish. This develops their willingness to pass more. I would say they initiated the passing more as they grew older. We started to develop passing and sharing skills way before any of us venture into playing sports.

If you think back to the last time you were playing with a child, passing was filled with laughter and excitement. I saw a video recently of a father and son drawing up a basketball play in their living room. The dad drew up the quick offensive set for him and his son to run. The end result was the dad throwing an alley-oop to the son for the dunk. If you ever saw someone throw an alley-oop before, I am sure you know the kind of excitement that transpired from the little boy after he dunked it home on his Fisher Price hoop. That wasn't the only thing about the video that stood out. At the end of the video, you can even hear the sister celebrating with her brother and father.

That is how passing and being unselfish works in life. I like to see it as a triangle model. The dad threw the lob, the son caught the alley-oop with assistance from the dad, and the sister was able to witness the magnificent assist. It feeds the spectator's spirit as well. They too want to be a part of passing and being unselfish. We see it all the time as adults. Passing and sharing impacts everyone.

At work, we were recently celebrating a special gift from a donor. The donor brought up the concept of "Impact Giving." His speech was so powerful. The donor talked about impacting the community and world and how those who taught him impacted his journey. What transpired was an extremely generous gift to his alma mater. Not only did he share his finances, but he shared his story. That is how passing works in life. When we make an assist, we are giving our friends and teammates an opportunity to impact the game and the lives of others.

There is a ton of joy in passing and being unselfish during those brief interactions. As we get older, it gets easy to forget some of the basic principles we were taught as children. We can get the same joy and excitement from passing and sharing as adults when we do it from a good place in our hearts. Donors share their wealth with nonprofits they are passionate about. Grandparents share wisdom with their grandkids. Motivational speakers share their experiences and motivation with the world. Educators share their passion, commitment, and love with their students. Coaches share their knowledge of the game with their players. Chefs share their recipes with their students. Passing and sharing the ball in basketball can lead to easy points and victories. Passing and sharing the ball in life can have similar outcomes, whether you are passing or sharing encouragement, life-skills, love, compassion, empathy, positive energy, insight, or knowledge. Even sharing in someone's pain can be a victory.

Coaches preach sharing the ball. I say, "Share your love." We are victorious when we share our smiles, our failures, our struggles, our past experiences, our energy, our fresh ideas, our honesty, our joy, and our best selves.

Passing the ball is even more imperative in times of pressure. We full-court pressed and trapped a lot growing up in Saginaw, Mich. It was a part of the culture, and we were good at it. I have also been on the other end of a good full-court press from an opposing team. Passing and sharing the ball in trap or pressure situations is pretty much life-or-death in basketball. Beating a trap and full-court press is easier said than done. Not even practice can simulate some full-court presses.

Life can sometimes feel like a full-court trap. Sometimes you feel like you are on an island by yourself in some full-court trap situations. Like basketball, in life, it is easy to forget we have teammates and people around us to help with the pressure. You may be saying, "I really do not have anyone." **(If that is you, please do not hesitate to reach out to me after reading this via email. awingard89@icloud.com)** We think we are better and stronger, and we try to beat the pressure by splitting the trap, which usually leads to a turnover. A full-court press and trap defensive scheme is meant to disturb your comfort zone and force you to make errors. You will make many errors during this life journey.

Pause and take time to reflect on the fundamentals of sharing and passing the ball.

Think back to the beginning of this chapter. Envision the smiles between you and the child you were playing catch with. Never forget that image when you are caught in a full-court press. Never forget that image when you have an opportunity to share something precious.

Passing also serves as a way to build trust among team members. When athletes pass the ball, they are telling their teammates they trust them. When we share our struggles with our close friends, we are saying, "I trust you. We are stronger together. I need my ride or die on this one." Trust serves as the foundation of our personal and business relationships. If you are getting ready to test your personal record on the bench, you are not going to ask someone to spot you who you do not trust. If you are sharing your relationship problems with someone, you are not going to share those relationship problems with someone who does not value his or her own relationship. If you want to enter the new year with better eating habits, you will seek a trusted nutritionist. Trust has to be developed in sports, as in every area of life. Trust isn't developed after one practice. It takes time. Every day we practice to build trust.

You have to be *willing* to share and pass the ball in basketball. You have to be *willing* to share and pass on this journey we call life. Arguably, this is the most important and lost concept when it comes to passing and sharing. Once, I read a headline from a sport column that said, "Sixers Willingness to Pass will be Key During the Playoffs." A great assist is not just for the person receiving the pass. That is the beauty of passing and sharing. Basketball is a team sport, and so is life.

Chapter Seven Wrap-Up: One More!

1. What is one thing you could share with someone this week?

2. What is one thing you could pass to someone this week?

3. Do you know anyone struggling with their confidence? How could you help them?

4. When was the last time it felt like all the walls were caving in on you? What did you learn from it? Who helped you during that time? Did you say "thank you"? If not, take time to say it now.

5. What are some drills you can do to prepare for the full-court press or trap life will throw at you?

CHAPTER EIGHT
TRIPLE THREAT

"Balance is not something you find, it's something you create." - Jana Kingsford

The triple threat position is as crucial as any move in the game of basketball. It is the most fundamental position for a ball handler and occurs when dribbling is not happening or when the ball handler is stationary moving only their pivot foot. This position allows the offensive player to have options as they plan their next move. The offensive player can pass, dribble, or shoot. For this move to be effective, the player must be balanced and have their head up, good posture, and a strong grip.

The defensive player plays a role in determining what the offensive player can do in their triple threat position. The offensive player has to read what the defense is giving them. If you are playing a team that prides themselves on their ball pressure, it is extremely important for the offensive player to be strong with the ball. Being strong with the ball also means you have a solid base for balance purposes. Otherwise, the defensive player will impose their will and force the offensive player's behavior to be dictated by them or, even worse, cause a turnover. We preyed on players who were weak with the ball. We knew we could dictate their behavior.

We face many adversaries on our daily walk that resemble the defender described above. Depression and anxiety prey on you when you turn your back. Fear and addiction prey on you when you are not balanced. Your peace is taken from you when you don't have your head up and eyes forward.

Other adversaries will take the form of a physical person. The individual could be trying to knock you off your pivot intentionally or unintentionally. We hope to avoid the situation or alleviate the pressure by turning our back, but that only makes the situation worse. When you first start playing basketball, that is a normal response to pressure. But all you will be doing is obstructing your vision and turning your back on your teammates, family, and friends. You need to pick your chin up and be strong with the ball. Swing an elbow across the face of adversity, pain, anxiety, and distraction to create some space. This will give you an opportunity to gather yourself and think about the right decision. Pressure defense comes at you fast in the game. Life will come at you fast as well. Especially when you least expect it.

The moment you turn your back or drop your head, you open yourself up to being overcome by adversity and pressure. Getting the offensive player to turn their back was a part of our defensive scheme. We forced the issue at times as defenders. We screamed "Trap house!" during the course of the game when we wanted to set up a trap and make the opposing team uncomfortable. It could be after a timeout, after they made basket, or in the middle of their offensive set. If we thought we could get a turnover and an easy basket, one or all of us would yell, "Trap house."

Head up, Eyes Forward

"Triple threat" is bigger than basketball jargon. The triple threat position is a life phrase. As I mentioned early in this chapter, the triple threat position consists of balance, posture, grip, and keeping your eyes up. I read a book a few years back where the author stated why he stopped drinking alcohol: he wanted to be more observant when he was around people. Head up and eyes forward. Being observant is one of the benefits of having your head up and eyes forward. I try to make a point of walking with my head up, and I always find it interesting that many do not do the same.

While walking across campuses around the country, I see many students faculty, and staff walking with their heads down. True, some people are unable to walk with their heads up due to injury or disability; however, many of the people I saw walking like this were physically distracted because they were looking down at their mobile phone. Others appeared lost in thought, while others may walk with their head down as a lack of confidence in themselves.

Hundreds, if not thousands, of studies provide evidence suggesting that walking is good for your health. I'd like to add that walking *with your head up and eyes forward* is more important to your physical and mental health. As a professional, walking with your eyes up is important for your business health. As a young adult, walking with your eyes up is vital to your mental health. One psychologist associated walking with your head down as a signal of weakness (unless you are physically unable, of course).

The 7/11 rule states that within 7 seconds people are making 11 assumptions about who you are. Our posture plays a big role in telling others about ourselves. When we walk around with our heads down, we are displaying poor posture, and we open ourselves up to elements around us that will not be beneficial for our health. We also magnify the current problems in our lives by creating seclusion when we aren't making eye contact as we walk. Anxiety is amplified when we seclude ourselves from the rest of the world. Fear is amplified when we seclude ourselves from the world. Loneliness is amplified when we seclude ourselves from the world. Plus, you don't see danger when you walk with your head down.

A few years ago, a video of a young lady texting and walking was circulating. She was walking with her head down and so engaged in the conversation on her mobile phone that she ran into a wishing well and fell in. Was it staged or real? No one knows. But it paints a vivid picture of what can result from walking with your head down.

Walking with your eyes up is a decision. Whether I am having a good day or a bad day, I tell myself to walk with my eyes up. It is my responsibility to make sure someone notices a smile or receives a greeting. When we see it as a responsibility, we take pride in walking with our head up. Someone is counting on us! Someone may be lonely and that greeting could be exactly what they need to keep pushing. That person could be walking with their head up intentionally looking for a light. You could be that light. If someone is struggling or worrying, your smile is exactly what they need to see to get through whatever they are battling.

Walking with our eyes up is a fundamental decision we start our day with. Walking is an active activity. So, why not be an "active walker"? Be present during your walk. Be present during your workday. Be present while you walk through the halls of your high school. Be present while you walk from your dorm to class.

It is easy to walk with our eyes up when we are traveling the world. We keep our eyes up because we don't want to miss anything cool. *What if we are missing something special in our own backyard?* What if we are missing loving relationships in our own backyard?

While writing this chapter, I started to reflect on my time working at Disney World in Orlando, Fla. During my orientation, I remember our orientation leader discussing the "Disney Experience" and what it entails. As cast members, we were responsible for providing a memorable experience for our guests, and we all took pride in that mission. One of the service guidelines includes making eye contact and smiling. Below are Disney's Seven Service Guidelines. I underlined and bolded the four that help express the importance of walking with your head up and eyes forward.

1. Be *Happy*...make eye contact and smile!
2. Be like *Sneezy*...greet and welcome each and every guest. Spread the spirit of hospitality...It's contagious!
3. Don't be *Bashful*...seek out guest contact.
4. Be like *Doc*...provide immediate service recovery.
5. Don't be *Grumpy*... display appropriate body language at all times.
6. Be like *Sleepy*...create dreams and preserve the "magical" guest experience.
7. Don't be *Dopey*...thank each and every guest!

I have countless examples of being an "active walker" during my Disney experience. Whether I was walking to the break room or clocking out for the day. Being present with my eyes up provided that "magical" guest experience, whether guests wanted me to take a family picture or asked where Casey's Corners was located. We can have that same kind of impact in our daily lives.

Head up and eyes forward. Having your chin up as an offensive player gives you the ability to see the entire floor. When you are facing the basket, you can see where the defensive players are located and identify open teammates and open lanes. Life is very similar. When your head is up, you can see opportunities when they present themselves.

Whether it is something small like cheering someone up with a smile or something massive like throwing the lob to a soaring teammate, co-worker, family member, or friend, when we go through life, keeping our head up and eyes forward as much as possible is fundamental. It not only presents us with opportunities, but it also gives us an opportunity to see things from a different perspective. In everything that we do, perspective is key.

In life, you never want to put yourself in a position with limited vision. As an offensive player, being able to see the entire floor is essential to your personal success and also your team's success. On our journey, we see our family members' and friends' success. I often tell my friends that the worst feeling is not being able to see. Those who wear glasses or contacts can relate to this next story. You get home from the gym after a long day at work and jump in the shower. You drift off into your thoughts in the shower and you lose track of time. You finally get out of the shower, and now you can't remember where you put your glasses. We are creatures of habit, so we know they can only be a few places. And now after a great shower to decompress, we are back to square one. When this happens to me, I am frustrated because I can't see, and I do not remember where I put my glasses. Frustration now turns into fear. What if I flop down somewhere and sit on them? What if they bounced off the bed and are laying on the floor, and I step on them? Limited vision is detrimental to us mentally. Limited vision produces frustration, which could lead to fear, anxiety, and a host of other elements that are not beneficial to us.

When the offensive player turns their back to the opposition, they only create more pressure and, most likely, a turnover. A turnover could lead to a fast-break ESPN Top 10 highlight. If you follow basketball, you know how those kinds of plays can shift the energy in the gym. The opposition gets under our skin and encourages us to turn our back, and what follows is normally a trap and turnover. At that point, the defender takes your joy, your energy, and your spirit. The same can be said for opposition in our lives. After those demoralizing plays, we don't feel like going to work, working out, falling in love again, or pursuing our dreams. Try really hard not to turn your back and keep your head up and eyes forward. I know that is easier said than done, but the effort alone will get you where you need to be. Chin up, chest up, and eyes forward!

Balance is Essential

If your head and eyes are down. I guarantee you are off balance. Balance is crucial for an effective triple threat position. Balance is also essential for our lives. Whether we are trying to balance our work life, relationships, eating habits, hobbies, passions, spiritual life, or our deep-rooted dreams, having a strong balance goes a long way in helping us in our lives.

You can be the strongest man alive and have poor balance. Balance, like everything else in basketball and life, can only be achieved through practice. We learn balance through different movements and circumstances surrounding our lives. Yoga is a great example of this. You can be an expert at one level and move to the next level and feel like you were duped by your instructor from the last class. I have been in that exact position. I walk into an advanced class only to realize my balance is atrocious. Creating and maintaining a strong balance is constant work. It is a daily walk.

Dr. Brad Manor, an instructor in medicine at Harvard Medical School stated, "We need careful planning of our movements, decision making, reaction time, and attention." Basketball players need careful planning of their next offensive move. Business professionals need careful planning of their next move. Teachers need careful planning of their next move. Parents need careful planning of their next move. A strong balanced triple threat position is vital to the success of a player. A strong balance is vital to us as humans.

We need careful planning of our decisions. We need careful planning of our next move. Whether you're deciding to move to a new career, move to a new city, move forward with your business plan, move forward with introducing the guy or girl to your family, move forward to ask for the gift, move forward to ask for a raise or title change, or move forward with purchasing a home, balance is essential when making decisions. When we are off-balance, we are liable to make a poor decision. Having a solid and sturdy base will help us make better decisions.

There is a reason the National Weather Service tells us to seek shelter in a cellar or basement when tornadoes are present. The foundation of a home is there. The foundation is strong, and we have a better chance of survival. The triple threat position is metaphorically our "foundation." When the storms of life are approaching, we should retreat and find comfort in our triple threat position.

How we react to certain situations is an indicator to how strong our foundation, core, base, and balance are at that time. When our balance is unstable, we become liable to react in a negative manner. Most people listen to respond instead of listening to digest. That is a sign of poor balance.

When you are balanced, you do not need to respond right away. Let the thought settle before responding. Many of us could have saved ourselves a lot of trouble by practicing balance in our personal lives as much as we did in the gym. Have you ever responded quickly to someone and later regretted? Have you ever responded to an email negatively and later regretted it? We allow our emotions to be quickly triggered, and we end up saying or doing something we did not necessarily care to even say. We allow others to influence our emotions, and we become quickly triggered.

In a normal situation, you know you would never say or do anything so reckless. But when you are not balanced, you make reckless decisions. I was watching the show *Iron Fist* one evening. One of the warriors was having a conversation at the table with a friend. The warrior started getting angry, but he did whatever he needed to do to regain his balance in the conversation. Without the proper balance, the situation could have turned for the worst. That is what having a strong balance can do in our lives. It keeps us grounded.

Medical professionals have spent many hours looking at the importance of balance as an athlete. Sport medical professionals have studied the correlation between balance and injury prevention. Two recent basketball-specific studies identified that, "just eight weeks (three 20–30 minute sessions per week) of proprioceptive and neuromuscular training (https://physioworks.com.au/treatments-1/proprioception-balance-exercises) can significantly reduce the risk and total number of ankle injuries over the season." I am a firm believer that balance is tied to injury prevention, as well as being more explosive.

As I got older and basketball became more intense, I noticed that my body was unable to handle the ground and pound of the game. I always assumed it was due to my lack of strength when I was younger. I am sure that played a small role in my injury history, but I truly believe it was my lack of balance. I rolled my ankles routinely during a normal basketball season. During my freshman year of college, my ankles finally had enough. Ice and rest wouldn't get me back on the court this time. I could barely walk, and at this point, my pain tolerance was slightly higher because of the frequent occurrence. So, I knew something was different. I went to the emergency room the following day, and the doctor confirmed that I had a microfracture in my ankle and would need surgery.

During the rehab process, I realized the importance of balance. I spent hours falling over. I was frustrated with myself, and I was frustrated that no one told me how important balance was growing up. It really is our foundation, and my foundation was horrendous! No wonder my body couldn't withstand the advancement of the game.

I spent all spring and early summer building my strength back up in a rehabilitation clinic. The results were unreal! Not only did I recover from my surgery fast, but I was stronger, more explosive, and faster than ever. Rehab with my physical therapist partnered with the great athletic training staff at Delta College had me ready for the season. My eyes were wide open at that point. I was all in on balance and understood how important it would be for my development as a player and a man.

Basketball moves fast, which means as a player, you always have to be attentive. If you aren't balanced and you see your teammate cutting quickly, you are liable to turn the ball over because your pass is weak and your accuracy is off. Nothing upsets a coach more than when a player jumps and tries to make a decision while gliding through the air. If you are balanced and strong with the ball, you will be more effective in your passing and decision making. When your friend needs advice but you are not balanced, what kind of advice are you going to be able to provide? Is your heart open to the conversation? Where is your mind? Will you be able to be the friend they need?

Just the other night, I was watching a college team playing in Chicago. The offensive team was taking the ball out of bounds under the opposing team's basket. The player passed it in-bounds to one of his teammates. The teammate took a couple dribbles, picked up the ball, and tried to pass the ball behind him to the point guard. Both offensive players were being pressured, and the guard who was passing the ball was not balanced. The guard was being pressured by the defender, and he was almost falling over due to the pressure. They ended up turning the ball over at a really crucial time in the game. Think about how drastic that could be for a friend who really needs an ear and a friend. Think about how drastic being unbalanced could be as a friend consults you about a decision they are preparing to make.

That exact basketball scenario has played out several times in my life. I was not balanced, and I made a poor decision. The bad part is, in life, you may not be able to blame any defenders for the turnover. The only person we can blame for being unbalanced is ourselves. Some of those poor decisions led to a turnover. Some of those poor decisions changed the dynamic of my day. Some of those poor decisions led to me blowing a sale. Some of those poor decisions led to me almost crippling positive relationships. Establishing a strong, balanced triple threat position is vital to the success of many basketball players. A strong balance is essential not only to our success as professionals but to our ability to survive and thrive.

Chapter Eight Wrap-Up: Triple Threat

1. What has knocked you off balance recently?

2. What happened after you were knocked off balance? Was there a ripple effect?

3. How did you respond?

4. What can you do to improve your balance? (As a friend, co-worker, etc.)

CHAPTER NINE
TAKE THE LAYUP,
SON...

"Take the layup, son." – Andrew Wingard

Easy baskets are always a great way to turn a bad game into a good one. Sometimes it works, and other times it does not. The goal is to prepare the best possible way you know. The last thing you want to do in that situation is force the issue. That only hurts you and your team more. When coaches see their players struggling, they sub that player out. Maybe, the athlete needs a breather. Maybe, the athlete is dealing with an issue outside of the game. Whatever it is, the coach is responsible for noticing the signs and helping his player out. Sometimes, that works, but at other times, it's just a bad day, and an easy basket is all we really need.

When you are starting a new position, the first 90 days are crucial. Whether you are stepping into a leadership role or entry-level position, attack the first 90 days with precision. If you have not faced any of these scenarios, you will. You may join an organization that has been running like a well-oiled machine and will not need your input right away. In those situations, it may be best to sit back and learn as much as possible. You may be coming into a situation where the previous person left on a high note. The last thing you want to do is come in and step on any toes right away. Ruffling feathers may not be the best use of your time during the first 90 days.

Then there are your code red scenarios, like when there was no predecessor or the guy before you left the ship sinking. In that situation, the organization is looking for quick results, and these situations can be stressful.

I have fortunately been able to see both sides of this. It doesn't matter if you are joining an organization with a strong core or an organization sinking looking for a life jacket. The first 90 days is crucial in either scenario. The first thing I look for are easy layups: the easy wins. Is there anything I can do right away to make an impact? I seek early wins for confidence but also to gain respect among my peers. In basketball, an easy layup could mean so much for the rest of the game. When I landed an easy basket early in the game, my confidence would rise, and that is all I needed to get moving. Work can be like that as well. That is why the first 90 days in your new role is so important. That is why easy layups are so important. It's great for the organization, and more importantly, it's great for you personally.

Chapter Nine Wrap-Up: Take the Layup Son!

1. What are some easy wins you can get done over the next 30, 60, 90 days? This could be for work, your personal life, or both. You will need more space than this notes section. Maybe create a PowerPoint to house your 30-, 60-, 90-day plan.

2. Ask your supporting cast what attributes you bring to the table. "What am I good at from your perspective?" Etc.

BONUS CHAPTER STEPPING OUTSIDE OF YOUR COMFORT ZONE

"Become comfortable being uncomfortable." –
Anonymous

Comfort zones are the daily routines that are regular, predictable, and cause no mental or emotional strain and stress. A comfort zone is not associated with only one race, ethnicity, culture, background, or social class. We all have one!

I will also say there is not anything wrong with staying inside of your comfort zone. Many professionals suggest leaving your comfort area, but that idea is not for everyone, much like college is not for everyone. It is like when you see something that says, "All couples should go skydiving together." You can't honestly expect that experience to engage everyone the same way.

Some people are more productive in their comfort zone. Some people are healthier in their comfort zone. We are only human, and we value comfort. Some would even say that "comfort" is the American dream, and that idea is hard to argue. Our comfort zone is a place of peace and order. The comfort zone only becomes a problem when you don't hold yourself accountable for your thoughts. If you have a dream of opening your own restaurant and you do not follow through on your thoughts, someone else will claim your vision, and you will most likely work for someone else's dream. That is when your comfort zone becomes an issue— when you don't seek to challenge yourself daily, or don't put yourself in situations to achieve your goals.

Why would I leave something that feels so good? It's silly, right? Who encourages people to leave something that is working and keeps me happy? This section may not be for you. You may be thinking that life is great right now and leaving your comfort zone is not something you need to do. If you feel that way, I urge you to reconsider what leaving your comfort zone really means. Leaving your comfort zone is more than leaving your physical destination. It means talking to people you disagree with or you don't share the same beliefs or values with. Leaving your comfort zone is trying a new recipe for dinner on Thursday night. Leaving your comfort zone is not tracking how many reps you do in the weight room. Leaving your comfort zone is asking more questions and responding less. Leaving your comfort zone is talking to the colleague that always seems to be upset. Leaving your comfort zone is reading a different genre of book. Leaving your comfort zone is traveling to a city or country to engage in their culture. Leaving your comfort zone is changing your routine. That last one can be really scary because we are creatures of habit. I can hear you now, "Change my routine? I think not, Andrew!"

I always found it interesting when I would hear conversations regarding inner city youth having the same opportunities as everyone else. Even if the idea had some truth, it ignores the concept of comfort zone. It ignores our basic instincts as humans to want to be around normalcy. It ignores the idea of being around loved ones. It ignores the idea of being around people who look like us. It ignores the idea of being around people who think like us. As a young adult, that is a terrifying idea. Many people will take comfort over something "better" because they are used to their current circumstances. Again, we are only human. Only those who are truly passionate about an idea or a goal will embrace the idea of leaving their comfort zone. Those individuals know the risk and are willing to sacrifice their comfort to meet a desired outcome.

Whenever I think of my comfort zone, I reflect on the idea of being in the wilderness. I recall the movie *300* and Leonidas's journey. Leonidas, a young boy, was taken from his mother and dropped into the wilderness. He was forced into the wild to defend himself and grow. He would either overcome his obstacles and return a Spartan or not return at all.

The keyword from the previous paragraph is "forced." Leonidas didn't willingly take himself out of his comfort zone. He was forced by the elders of Sparta. That could represent your parents, your pastor, your mentor, a high school teacher, coaches, or close friends. His support team understood what was at stake. Leonidas needed to grow.

Leaving our comfort zone does not have to be a solo mission like Leonidas'. It may seem that way when you think about leaving your comfort zone, but it does not have to be that way. I won't lie and say there won't be times when you feel like young Leonidas out in the wilderness roaming around, but, of course, this is the modern day, and we have access to people at the touch of a button. You may have to recreate your core when you leave your comfort zone, but that is one of the bonuses of leaving your comfort zone. We need people in our corner. Whether they are encouraging us to venture out into the wilderness or being a friend during the uncomfortable season.

When I consider the type of people we should surround ourselves with during the process of leaving our comfort zone, I immediately see my former strength and conditioning coaches.

Strength coaches are trained professionals in getting you out of your comfort zone. Strength coaches are hired to decrease the risk of injury, get their clients bigger, faster, and stronger and more importantly to build their character. All these conditions are only obtainable through vacating our comfort zone.

One more! Push through! Hold it! Drive! Finish! You might hear a strength coach reciting those words throughout their workday. Strength coaches enjoy pushing the envelope with their clients or athletes because they know physical, mental, and personal development are at the end of the tunnel. One college strength coach said, "We separate the men from the boys during the off season." Their job is all about getting athletes outside of their comfort zone to help them be the best they can be.

Strength coaches are also teachers, mentors, and motivators. Strength coaches are experts in increasing confidence and self-esteem in their clients and athletes. Confidence and self-esteem are crucial when you are away from your comfort zone. When you develop confidence in yourself, you will see yourself in a different light: you will start to change. Your self-talk will change. The way you tackle your day will change. That is why confidence is so powerful.

Everyone has their own way of building up confidence. Shelly Raube and her student assistants helped create me during my time at Delta College. Strength coaches have a way of helping us redefine how we perceive ourselves, and they play an integral role in restructuring how we think. We say, "maybe," but strength coaches say, "You got this." So, make sure you have that type of individual in your corner. Whether that is a pastor, a janitor, your neighbor, a professor, or even your boss, you need these people to help you not only see yourself in a different light but to encourage you when you are close to giving up.

Leaving your comfort zone is not a painless activity. Which is why most shy away from the idea of leaving it. When we step outside of our comfort zone, we open ourselves up to stress and anxiety. We open ourselves up to failure. With that being said, you don't want to quickly get so far outside of your zone that the stress is overwhelming and you fall apart. As I mentioned earlier in this book, small actions and small steps are more important than taking big leaps.

Stepping outside of the defined comfort zone reminds me of a horror film. The one that always pops into my head due to me being a fisherman is *Lake Placid*. It's one of the reasons I was terrified about fishing in Louisiana by myself. The idea made me extremely uncomfortable because I do most of my fishing from the bank. I knew there was a risk, and I wasn't bold enough to leave my comfort zone during that time of my life. It makes me sad because I missed out on some good fishing in the bayou due to my fear, but I am also happy to still be alive. On the other end of the horror spectrum, we find ourselves lost in the woods running from a masked assailant, and at some point our mentality switches. We stop running and start fighting back. We come face to face with our fears, and all the stress and anxiety throughout the movie turns you into an absolute BEAST.

Leaving the defined comfort zone reminds me a lot of the surgery process. Have you ever had surgery? What did it do to your routine? Were you uncomfortable during the healing process?

Like surgery, leaving your comfort zone does not guarantee success, but it is very important that you have your own definition of success. Some people have surgery to strengthen a weak part of their body. I had surgery on my fractured ankle to get back to running and jumping. Anything less than that would not have been a success for me. Whereas others have surgery to have their comfort restored. Your definition of success and my definition will be drastically different. It is your responsibility to define what success means to you.

In 2015, I had a weird pull to start reading and writing. Two things I never really enjoyed. The urge was unique, and I could not quite grasp where it was coming from. So, I decided to leave my comfort zone. That following year, I read a few books and started a professional blog. I was extremely uncomfortable putting my thoughts into the world. But then I realized what could happen once I left my comfort zone. I reflected on my past comfort zone experiences. Once I stepped out and developed my blog, I took a leap of faith and started writing. Five years later, I started writing this book to share my personal thoughts and experiences with you. It was not always comfortable, but it was worth it.

There are many ways to expand your horizons and challenge your comfort zone, right in your current space. So take a small step and leave your comfort zone. Find a new recipe online and make it. Write the first page of your business plan. Have a conversation with someone of a different ethnicity. Spend five more minutes in the gym for one week. Reach out to a professional on LinkedIn to connect. Try the new restaurant down the street. Take a salsa dancing class. Buy a new book, and read ten pages. Ask your neighbor to sit down over a cup of coffee. Trying new things can be scary, but it can also give you a fresh new perspective.

Bonus Chapter Wrap-Up: Comfort Zone

1. How do you build up your confidence?

2. I talked about small steps briefly in this chapter. Are there any small steps you can take over the next seven days to pursue a goal you have had on your mind for a while?

3. What is your personal definition of success?

REFERENCES

Abella, Amanda. (2017, April 7). *6 Reasons Why Business Owners Should Focus on Follow-Ups.* Due. https://due.com/blog/follow-ups/.

Alvarez, Kim. (2015). *Customer Service with a Heart [PowerPoint Slides].* Retrieved from https://cdn.ymaws.com/www.taspa.org/resource/ resmgr/Summer_Conference_2015/Customer_S ervice-The_Disney_.pdf.

Dyer, Wayne. (2010). *The Power of Intention: Learning to Co-create Your World Your Way.* Hay House Inc.; Gift, Reissue Edition.

Felton, Julia. *The Importance of Follow Through.* BusinessHorsePower. https://www.businesshorsepower.com/the-importance-of-follow-through/.

Healthbeat. "Body and brain are crucial to good balance." Harvard Health Publishing. https://www.health.harvard.edu/healthbeat/body-and-brain-are-crucial-to-good-balance.

Meyer, Joyce. (2013). *Making Good Habits, Breaking Bad Habits: 14 New Behaviors That Will Energize Your Life*. FaithWords.

Schawbel, Dan. (2018, November 13). "Why work friendships are critical for long-term happiness." CNBC. https://www.cnbc.com/2018/11/13/why-work-friendships-are-critical-for-long-term-happiness.html.

Snyder, C. R., Rand, K. L., & Sigmon, D. R. (2002). "Hope theory: A member of the positive psychology family." In C. R. Snyder & S. J. Lopez (Eds.), Handbook of positive psychology (p. 257–276). Oxford University Press.

Stark, Rachel. "When the playing days end." *Champion Magazine: NCAA,* Spring 2018, http://www.ncaa.org/static/champion/when-the-playing-days-end/. Accessed 29 May 2020.

THANK YOU

This book is a small, detailed journal of my personal and professional experiences through the first thirty-one years of my life.

I would like to thank—

Close friends who read over chapters leading up to its release.

Cori Wamsley for editing my first book.

Rob W. for the cover design concept.

Everyone who has been a part of this beautiful life journey.

Most of all, my parents and siblings for the memories we have shared over the years and their unconditional love and support.

ABOUT THE AUTHOR

 Andrew Wingard is a professional fundraiser in the nonprofit sector. Andrew was born and raised in Saginaw, Mich. He obtained a bachelor's degree in business administration from Saginaw Valley State University (University Center, Mich.). Upon completing his coursework for his undergraduate degree, Andrew went to work for Walt Disney World in Orlando, Fla. as an intern. After completion of the Disney Program, he attended Western Kentucky University (Bowling Green, Ky.) where he obtained a master's degree in sport administration with a focus in intercollegiate athletics.

Andrew has worked for higher education institutions such as Western Kentucky University, Vanderbilt University, Texas Tech University, Tulane University, and Youngstown State University. Andrew's education and experience have provided opportunities for him to give back to athletes and local communities. Andrew currently lives in Youngstown, Ohio.

Made in USA - Kendallville, IN
1222217_9780578797854
01.06.2021 0838